ROOM AT THE TOP

ROOM AT THE TOP
— GOLF THE TORRANCE WAY —

BOB TORRANCE

WITH

NORMAN MAIR

FOREWORD BY

SEAN CONNERY

MAINSTREAM
PUBLISHING

Copyright © Bob Torrance with Norman Mair, 1989

First published in Great Britain in 1989 by
MAINSTREAM PUBLISHING COMPANY (EDINBURGH) LTD
7 Albany Street, Edinburgh EH1 3UG

ISBN 1 85158 096 4 (cloth)

British Library Cataloguing in Publication Data
Torrance, Bob
    Room at the top : golf the Bob Torrance way.
    I. Title   II. Mair, Norman
    796.352'3

ISBN 1-85158-096-4

Typeset in 11 on 13pt Imprint by Bookworm Typesetting Ltd., Edinburgh
Printed in Yugoslavia by Gorenjski Tisk, Kranj.

"I know all about the respectable, even remarkable, distances players have hit the ball standing on one leg, sitting in a chair or kneeling. They do not surprise me but neither do they alter the fact that I have seen every great player from Harry Vardon either on film or live and one thing they all had in common was good weight transference."

Bob Torrance.

Acknowledgements

Our grateful thanks go to Dave Cannon, Mike Cox, Peter Dazeley, Keith Hailey, Matthew Harris, Stewart Kendall, Lawrence Levy, William S. Paton, Phil Sheldon, Lauren St John, David Stranock, and David Varley for the use of the photographs in this book.

CONTENTS

FOREWORD

by SEAN CONNERY

I was once asked whether, if I had the choice, I would rather win an Oscar or the Open. Though my thespian friends might well have been shocked, I unhesitatingly nominated the latter.

Yet I was in my mid-thirties before I took the game up and then only because I had to look the part for the golfing scenes inseparable from the James Bond role in *Goldfinger*.

I had the advantage of being well built and enough of an athlete and ball-player to have signed professionally as an outside-right with Bonnyrigg Rose in the then fiercely competitive world of Scottish junior football. Indeed, when I was in the chorus of *South Pacific* and the football team drawn from the cast was under the patronage of Matt Busby and afforded the facilities of Old Trafford, there was even talk of my having a trial with Manchester United.

Celtic were my team and such as Jimmy Delaney and Charlie Tully my heroes. So much was it part of my life that when the time came for me to move from Bruntsfield Primary to Boroughmuir, I insisted on going to Darroch because they played football whereas Boroughmuir played rugby. Ironically, I have changed my mind about rugby over the years. Both my sons played it and I have come to see it as a grand game with a spirit of its own and one which is still free of so many of the ills which sadly have come to afflict soccer.

I had some golf lessons at Stoke Poges when preparing for *Goldfinger*, but not all that many, and if I had my time again I would do it properly and do what Albert Finney did. He took lessons for a month and more and, I understand, did not set foot on a golf course in the sense of playing a round until he had had the foundations of the swing solidly implanted.

I did the introduction to a John Jacobs instructional video and got the odd tip from him at various clinics. However, they were but brief encounters and my besetting sin of coming over the top became ever more deeply ingrained. With so grievous a flaw and unable to generate much in the way of distance, I leaned heavily on a good short game and the fact that I was naturally a tenacious competitor. What I never lacked from the first was keenness but though I played a lot, I did not in those days do much in the way of proper practice which was perhaps just as well since, prior to encountering Bob Torrance, I should merely have been grooving faults.

My first contact with Bob stemmed from an article I read about him by John Hopkins in the *Sunday Times*. Liking both the sound of him and what he had to say, I wrote to him and, as anyone who knows him will probably have guessed, he offered to look over my swing at the first opportunity.

It came at a BBC pro-celebrity series at Turnberry and I shall never forget how, after we had repaired to the practice ground, he startled me by enquiring whether my copy of Ben Hogan's *Modern Fundamentals* was in the car or my hotel room. He had seen at once what I was trying to do but was soon explaining that, incomparable striker though Ben Hogan had been, his way was not for me.

The ideal swing, he said, would be in the form of a vertical wheel but because of the way a player has to stand to the ball that wheel has to be tilted, though nowhere near as horizontally as mine was. Mainly by working on my posture, he soon had me swinging on a much more upright plane with the club more on line at the top. Once that was achieved, he set about improving my leg action and my weight shift.

Now, the key thought Bob has given me is to have the feeling of my left shoulder pointing behind the ball at the top of my

Seve Ballesteros just past impact. Note weight on the left side, right foot working, left arm rotating through impact rather more rapidly than usual for this particular shot. Position of the head is exemplary.

backswing and I find that if I get into the position at that point which he wants, I get on the right side to the appropriate degree without having to think about it. Thereafter, it is all more a matter of automatic reaction and release than of any further conscious swing thoughts.

He uncorked in me some 30 or 40 yards I had never had before and I would judge my better drives to average out around the 260 yards mark. My handicap at the R & A is ten and yet, thanks to Bob, I went round the Old Course in a gross 69 *en route* to winning the Jubilee Vase – a feat which not so long before would have been about thrice as impossible as the most outrageous of James Bond's. Moreover, since I can bracket it with the Calcutta Cup I won over the New Course, I now have a golfing double of which I am immodestly proud.

Bob works with what you have got, keeps it simple and has what in many another walk of life would more readily be recognised as flair.

Only a few years ago he was just Sam Torrance's father, the professional-cum-green-keeper at the public course of Routenburn in Largs. Today, the most famous names in golf beat a path to his door, and yet his fame as a teacher has spread not by lavish projection in golfing magazines or expensive advertising, but simply by word of mouth on the part of a gratefully appreciative and growing clientèle.

I count myself lucky to be among their number and so I cannot but applaud Bob's decision to commit to paper, in *Room at the Top*, his insight into the technique of the greatest game mankind has yet devised.

INTRODUCTION
by SAM TORRANCE

My father has been my sole teacher. Indeed, it is one of my greater satisfactions that having the swing he gave me in the shop window, in the sense of being on the professional tour, is always said to have sown the seeds of the enviable reputation he now enjoys as a teacher.

He has, as I think any teacher who would aspire to be great has to have, a real feel and love for the game. He has, too, at least when he knows that the pupil himself is genuinely interested in improving, endless patience.

An eye for technique is something he has always had and, since he believes that you never stop learning, his knowledge of his subject has grown markedly in recent years when he has had more opportunity to study the outstanding players of the world scene at first hand, to rub shoulders with them and to talk theory.

His oft-reiterated coaching creed is, "Never interfere with nature, never weaken the strong to strengthen the weak." In accordance with that philosophy, he is essentially a coach who teaches not a swing but the person. He would never, for instance, attempt to have an Eamonn Darcy swinging like a Seve Ballesteros but would instead work around the obvious good points in Eamonn's somewhat unconventional action.

Again, he never merely points out a flaw but traces it back to its origin. Let's say that I have got a bit shut at the top of the backswing. He would track it all the way back until he found the cause and then show me, say, how a fault in my takeaway was dictating the position of the club-face at the top of the swing. A bonus stemming from that approach is, of course, that he takes the pupil with him in that the player understands the wherefore and the why.

Although he does not teach a swing as such, he is a devout believer in the importance of the fundamentals and getting them right. Above all, the basis of his teaching is footwork, the action of the feet, legs and hips. To my mind, there are twin benefits accruing from that approach in that you do not have to have certain physical attributes to conform to his teaching, while the swing he gives you, however different from the next man's, has been built to last far beyond the muscular and pliable days of youth into a player's later years.

His label nowadays, and it is one of which I am probably as proud as he is, is that of the pros' pro but I have hardly seen a golfer whom he could not have hitting the ball well in an hour. His thinking on the swing and the emphasis he places on certain key aspects of it, as revealed in this book, will surely help many.

Finally, my father counts himself very fortunate to have had as his collaborator on *Room at the Top*, Norman Mair, a talented sportsman in his own right and a golf writer for whose knowledge and understanding of the swing he has long had the greatest admiration and respect.

ONE

THE ROAD TO OKLAHOMA

Airborne *en route* to Oak Tree in Oklahoma as personal coach to Ian Woosnam for the USPGA championship hardly constitutes space travel. Nevertheless, as Manchester Airport was left far behind in our slipstream, I could not but reflect that this was light years away from the life I used to lead – and would maybe largely still be leading had my son Sam not had an eye for a golf-ball or even perhaps if he had been 25 yards shorter.

Rather than, in the vernacular of golf, making a two-tee start to my story, let me go back to the beginning . . ..

I did not swing a golf-club until I was 16 and even then, somewhat improbably, only because of the sacrosanct place which used to be accorded Sunday lunch in so many Scottish homes. My sister's husband, the late Sandy McClellan, a good golfer who played to a four handicap, was having a round one Sunday morning with my father and I was sent up to the club to make sure that they did not linger too long in the bar to the ruination of the Sunday roast.

As I arrived, they were on the 17th where Sandy hit his tee shot into the rough, cursing because it was a brand new ball and would be difficult to locate. I went straight to it and Sandy, as surprised as he was grateful, exclaimed to me that with an eye like that I ought to have a shot myself. He handed me his hickory-shafted cleek and, to no one's amazement more than my own, I produced an absolute beauty, the sensation of the shaft bending and the ball on the club-face being with me to this

A young Bob Torrance with his first boss, Jock McKellar, the professional at the Largs Golf Club. "He was the hardest of taskmasters," recalls Bob Torrance, "but very fair. I could not have got a better early grounding."

day. That one fix was enough to have me helplessly hooked – your proverbial golfing junkie.

It was curious, in a way, that I had not previously tried my hand at golf because my father, Sam Torrance Mark I, after his days as a booth boxer drew to a close, was a very keen golfer even though he was about as wide as he was tall, five feet either way.

Like many another foot-loose, fancy free and cheerfully feckless teenager, I had experimented gingerly with various forms of employment, including that of market gardener. Now, though, I suddenly had a real purpose in life and I practised morning, noon and evening, getting down to scratch in three years.

There came a day, however, when I met June, now my wife, in a cafe. Having sent the young man she was dating packing, I was soon courting her with much the same enthusiasm as I had been practising my golf. In fact, for a spell, I even turned my back on the game – something which would have appalled P. G. Wodehouse's "Oldest Member" and which, across the years, now shocks me.

June could be excused if she were to claim now that I gave her a totally false impression, for in no time at all I was back living the game almost every daylight hour, having taken on the job of assistant at Largs Golf Club. My boss, Jock McKellar, was a hard taskmaster but very fair and I adored the environment from the very first.

My day began at eight o'clock and, since I was not just the assistant professional but an assistant green-keeper, I had to cut around a dozen greens on my own with a hand machine. In the afternoons, the machinery had to be oiled and cleaned, after which it was time to wade barefoot into the creek which threaded the course and clean out by hand the weed which grew there – and a tough and adhesive species it proved to be. By five in the evening, it was home for tea but I still had to come back up to man the shop and dispense the green-fee tickets. Add in that another of my duties was to wash, clean and oil the caddy-cars, and, in the summertime, it was sometimes 11 o'clock at night before I knocked off.

Old McKellar had a moped which could not cope with the final ascent to the clubhouse and every morning I would go down to the gate to push it the rest of the way, keeping half an eye on McKellar whose first action was invariably to count the caddy-cars and inquisitively spin a wheel to check that they had been oiled.

It was a crowded schedule but in the winter I still always made time to saw some logs, which I would rope together and string round my neck before cycling home. I earned a far from princely five pounds a week and coal was well beyond our pocket, our in-house entertainment being nothing so grand as television but merely Radio Luxembourg.

When I first became addicted to the game, I managed to garner the few bob needed to purchase a copy of Byron Nelson's *Winning Golf* and I devoured every page, every line, and fondly thought that I was successfully emulating the action photographs. Yet, for all the rapidity with which I improved, I generated no real yardage and, try as I might, simply could not

*Bob Torrance with Jack Cordingley, an invaluable friend during
Bob's days as the Rossendale professional.*

work out why. The turning-point came when I attended a
professional tournament at Prestwick and the very first
professional I saw hitting a drive made me realise how little of
what he had was in my own swing. Even then I could quickly
detect that the difference lay in the way he started the
downswing and in the subsequent – and, in truth, consequent –
use he made of his legs. I could not wait to get back to
Routenburn and incorporate those movements into my own
swing.

While I was at Largs, I was invited to play in an exhibition
match at Routenburn, partnering John Panton against Eric
Brown and Alex MacGregor, a crack amateur who had lost to
Dr Frank Deighton in the final of the 1956 Scottish Amateur
championship. There was no question with McKellar of his
allowing me time off to practise, though he did excuse me from
the cleaning of the burn in the days before the match. If
memory serves me aright, Panton and I won by something like
5 and 4. I think I went to turn in 31 but what hurt, because there
was a money prize for the best individual score, was that I
finished with two pars against Eric Brown's eagle and birdie, a
67 to his 66.

The late Bill Howard (right), than whom Bob Torrance never had a better friend, receives the Captain's Prize at Rossendale from the club President, Derek Ingham.

At the age of 27 I was appointed as professional and head greenkeeper to Rossendale, a nine-hole course in Lancashire where I inherited as my green-keeping staff a wonderful old chap by name of Dick Lamb. Now my day's work began at six o'clock, Old Dick cutting the fairways while I attended to the greens, the aprons, the surrounds, the tees and the bunkers. We had a cart which could hold no more than a ton of stuff and an ancient Ferguson tractor which, by then, would have been hard pressed to take the top off an egg. Yet, in my years at Rossendale, the venerable Dick and I built nine new tees and around five new greens.

Again, I enjoyed every minute of it, though to many an outsider it might have seemed tantamount to slave labour, for even then my weekly wage was just nine pounds. June and I,

Tony Jacklin (centre) and Bob Torrance respond as Ireland's Eamonn Darcy heroically puts his Ryder Cup past behind him to hole the last-green putt which beat Ben Crenshsaw in Europe's triumph in the 1987 Ryder Cup at Muirfield Village.

together with young Sam, were still living close to the breadline but we soon had some great friends among the members, including Jack Cordingley, who was a good player in his own right, and Bill and Jean Howard.

Very sadly, Bill is no longer with us but I shall never forget how, when we were going out to dinner as a foursome, he would mutter that I could not go out in public with him looking like that, straightening my tie and adjusting my pocket handkerchief – and afterwards I would find in my breast pocket a £20 note or even, on occasion, £50. It was Bill who taught me how to drive a car but it was Jack, whom I always understood to be the longest-established Austin agent in the country, who lent me assorted vehicles, from his own silver Rolls-Royce with which June and I once startled the attendant at the local cinema

Bob Torrance, the Scottish Golf Union's official coach, working under the sun at Duquesa in Spain with Scotland's top amateur squad. The player to whom he is giving advice is Jim Milligan, who went on to win the 1988 Scottish Amateur championship.

to the old van without a heater in which we made the long drive north to Largs.

We set off at two in the morning: June, myself, Sam, the dog and a hand mower I was taking back with me to a chum in Largs. It was so cold on that frost-ridden night that we had to stop every 40 or so miles to get out and exercise simply to get warm. It took us some eight hours but, on arrival in Largs, I headed straight up to Routenburn where, even though I was a professional, they allowed me to play in the monthly medals. After a few drinks with my pals, I sallied forth and shot 60, missing an eminently holeable putt on the last green for a 59. Not that, as a coach, I would recommend my pre-round preparation.

A wife with a licence to club her husband . . . June Torrance caddying for Bob on one of his relatively rare forays into tournament golf.

At Rossendale, too, I was invited to play in the monthly medals. Players like Harry Weetman and Dai Rees came to Rossendale to play exhibitions but 70 had never been broken there for 18 holes until I had a 66, my framed card being still up on the wall when last I was there.

I did quite well in various local events and, by coming second to Ted Large in the Northern Professional Championship, I qualified for the *News of the World* PGA Match-Play Championship at Turnberry, where I clocked in to find Eric Brown's caddie running a pencil through all those contenders who could not conceivably be a danger to his man, myself included. I was drawn against golf's Gentle Persuader, Ken Bousfield, but opened with three birdies in the first four holes to be three up on the fourth tee, receiving some distinctly colourful encouragement from Eric Brown as he passed by. In the end, Bousfield, with that beautiful short game of his, beat me, but at least I had given him a game.

Another highlight of my years at Rossendale was playing in

June Torrance in the overlapping grip of Terry Wogan, a great supporter of pro-am golf for charity.

the Piccadilly Medal at Hillside and, extraordinarily enough, on the practice ground of the inaugural Volvo Seniors British Open, I found myself next to Tom Innes with whom I had been paired at Hillside. The outstanding memory of the Piccadilly has to be of Jack Nicklaus who, as chance had it, was playing in the match immediately behind ours. I could not believe the distance he was hitting it and so often was he inadvertently in among us after we had played our seconds, we almost began to run. I recall crying to Tom, "This is getting bloody dangerous – they should have given us steel helmets!" I was holding forth afterwards on the incredible yardage Nicklaus had been getting when I felt a tap on the sleeve. "Jack," said the interjector, gently, "was driving with his three-wood!"

I watched Nicklaus during the Piccadilly whenever I could and, flying right elbow or not, I thought he was magnificent. Mark you, I finished a stroke ahead of him, which I always say is my one real claim to fame as a player.

June and I got on so well with almost everyone at Rossendale that it was a nasty jolt when the captain said that he wanted a word with me in the committee room. There was a short hole at Rossendale with a lot of dead ground in the form of a valley. There was an out-of-bounds behind the green and Rossendale golfers were no different from others in that they were always striving to get up with one club less than the next man. Accordingly, a great many tee shots spun back down the slope and what Sam and the other little brigands had been doing was hiding in the bushes, nipping out to cover the ball or balls with grass clippings and then ducking back to hide anew. If the golfer found his ball, well that was game, set and match to him, but if he passed on his way leaving it behind, they considered it the legitimate spoils of victory. The captain and his committee, of course, saw it very differently, taking a much sterner view and, since it was liable to be interpreted by nine members out of ten as theft, so too did I. Everyone knows what they say now about corporal punishment but the punishment I meted out to Sam did the trick.

From that day forth, though he was still just a wee boy, he seemed to see golf in a new light and there came an afternoon – and he can have been no more than nine – when he announced that he had gone round Rossendale's nine holes in 43. The holes at Rossendale were by no means short and I told him not to talk such nonsense but he stuck doggedly to his story and, in the end, he dragged me out on the grounds that seeing is believing. He went round in exactly the same score of 43 and I was duly impressed.

In 1963 I returned to Largs to accept the post of professional-cum-green-keeper at Routenburn, taking up my appointment earlier than originally envisaged in order to get the course into shape for an exhibition match featuring Eric Brown, John Panton, Dorothea Somerville and Belle Robertson. Sam's golf was now beginning to take a central place in our lives and I can see him yet on the first tee at the age of 11 in the Ayrshire Boys' championship. They called his name. I saw his face tighten in a

With Sam absent overseas, Bob and June Torrance accept the Skol Sportsman of the Year trophy on his behalf from the company's managing director, John Mackenzie.

frown of concentrated determination and he smashed it far down the fairway, his swing having had that all-important hit in it virtually from his days as a toddler.

I can remember Alex MacGregor, who had become something of a boon companion, observing during the Viking Cruise, a competition at Largs, that he had heard all about my son but had never seen him play. He was about to go forth, watch him and deliver his own verdict. An hour later he returned: "Superb, the best for his age I have seen."

Sam played in the Scottish Boys' Championship at North

Berwick but did not win it, though he reached the semi-final where he was stopped by the eventual champion, Russell Weir. The next time they met head to head was when they were professionals and were tied going into the last round of the Skol Golf and in this instance it was Sam who triumphed.

A Scottish Boys' internationalist, Sam turned professional at 16. Of course, the origins of my own reputation as a teacher were founded in Sam's swing and not least in what Jack Nicklaus described, after they had played three rounds together in the 1987 Open at Muirfield, as his "lovely tempo".

Yet, even as Sam was beginning to make a name for himself, I was drinking myself into oblivion. I drank scarcely at all until I was around 23 and even then for long enough drank only on Friday nights because that was all I could afford. Gradually it became one night after another until I was downing a bottle of whisky a day. There were two years when the problem was acute and I must have been the despair of my friends. Even June herself was affected, if only on the lines of the old saying that if you can't beat 'em, join 'em.

Some 12 or 13 years ago, I was sitting having my dinner, not drunk but having had a few, when I had an alcoholic seizure which not only abruptly ended my meal but very nearly terminated my life. I collapsed, turning the colour of Al Jolson, and poor June was reduced to hysterics.

I was saved by a quirk of fate in that one of the members who was at the club that night was an ambulance man and he saw that I had, to all intents and purposes, swallowed my tongue and was choking to death. He stuck some form of pin into it and retrieved it. Shortly the doctors arrived and had me transferred to hospital, their unequivocal warning being that either I gave up drinking or I would be dead within a couple of years, maybe even within one.

You don't, as they say, get two gypsy warnings in this life, and I stopped drinking there and then, my only real lapse thereafter occurring one winter at New Year, when I prevailed upon the barman to slip some vodka into my soda and lime.

When Sam turned up, I denied it hotly, knowing that you can't taste the vodka in such a drink, my fingers clamped like steel to the bar rail. But Sam knew . . ..

I am well aware that many an authentic alcoholic would say the same but I do not consider myself one because one drink does not set me off. I could happily pour the next one down the sink. On the other hand, I would freely admit to having been a bad drunk in the sense of being an argumentative one who was always getting into fights, both my nose and my jaw having been broken along the way.

When I called a halt to my drinking, I told June that it would not worry me if she had a drink, not add fatally to the temptation. But June, typically, partnered me in this as in all else.

Whether I can rightly be classed as an alcoholic or not, I believe devoutly that a man like Jimmy Greaves, who has been to the bottom of the bottle and back, is right to talk unashamedly of the darker years. Today I am as a man transformed and not just because I have found in teaching the fulfilment which eluded me as a tournament player. After all, a man of twelve and a half stones feels very different from one of eighteen, which was what I was when it seemed that almost all I did between drinks was eat.

Not too many are vouchsafed a second chance and I like to think that I have made the most of mine.

Sam Torrance in what he still sees as his finest hour – acknowledging the thunderous ovation of the galleries at The Belfry after holing the putt which simultaneously finished off Andy North, the US Open champion, and gave Europe the 1985 Ryder Cup.

TWO

A CASE IN POINT

by SAM TORRANCE

The right index finger pointing down the shaft, I am told, used to be known as the "After-40 finger" other than, for obvious reasons, in women's golf. But to me it was just something I picked up from watching Seve Ballesteros for whose putting stroke I have come to have a very healthy respect.

Because my father taught me so well, and because I have such faith in his doctrine, I have never felt the need, even when away on tour, to seek out other teaching professionals but, of course, you are learning all the time on the tour, often almost without knowing it. You assimilate not only the technique required for certain shots, and for various combinations of lie and stance, but also little points, often not much more than idiosyncrasies and personal mannerisms.

As a boy, for example, I copied Gary Player's version of the forward press, including that kicking-in of the right knee prior to the takeaway, but I have dispensed with it over the years, partly because my would-be replica had become, in my father's eyes, something of a two-piece duplicate.

Similarly, but more lastingly, I borrowed from Jack Nicklaus the practice of not grounding the club at the address, which not only prevents it from snagging on any little obstruction on the way back but helps to achieve a properly free and flowing start to the backswing. Such celebrated golfers as Greg Norman in the professional sphere and Michael Bonallack in the amateur successfully worked it into their own games but for all that I have used it for by far the greater part of my days on the tour, I am now trying to rid myself of the habit. I have come to the conclusion that it can breed inconsistency because, whereas the ground is the ground, you can never be quite sure whether your club is a quarter of an inch off the turf, half an inch, an inch or even not far short of a couple of inches. That can have a knock-on effect in terms of both path and plane in the ensuing swing.

Professionals can be very generous in the help they give each other, though my father always laughs at the day that Nick Faldo called across the fairway for my dad's phone number and I retorted that I had forgotten it!

No one holes everything and the professionals sometimes wince at how so many outside the tour or on its periphery see the game within a game that is putting. Nick Faldo struck the ball so well in 1988 and gave himself so many chances that, like such as Henry Cotton and Ben Hogan before him, he had the galleries and some of the pundits shaking their heads at the number of birdies that got away. To a degree, great striking is always liable to cast a much less favourable light on a man's putting than the sheer necessity of tenacious scrambling.

Not, of course, that anyone, least of all Nick himself, is denying that he has not putted as well as in the past or that he has not missed rather too many of the three- and four-footers, even allowing that one or two of those are always going to escape. Just that so many critics are blissfully oblivious to relative standards. Many of those who were at Oak Tree for the USPGA Championship, or who saw it in television, could hardly wait to recount afresh how badly Faldo had putted; and yet how many of them, even though they may well be very good putters at their own level, could have gone round those greens and only once taken three putts in 72 holes as I understand Nick did?

Towards the close of 1987 and on into 1988, I had my troubles on the putting green. Mark McNulty, nowadays listed as playing out of Zimbabwe, gave me what I suspect was very sound advice – namely, to forget all the suggested quick cures with their smack of golfing quackery and get right back to basics: "Square up your stance and your whole putting address, get the ball off the left heel and just concentrate on stroking it solidly."

In my view, Nick Faldo still heads the list as the greatest putter of my time, the man with the best stroke and certainly the one I should most like to own. Seve Ballesteros and Ben Crenshaw are both very good and both different but Faldo's whole putting action, from set-up and stance right through to the stroke itself, is in my eyes well-nigh perfect. I shall be amazed if his comparative fall from grace on the greens in 1988 proves much more than a temporary hiccup.

If Faldo is, year in, year out, the player I should most want to have putting for me, Bernhard Langer would be my choice in the so-called "cone of contention" – from 100 yards in, including the pitches and chips around the green and the greenside bunker recoveries. The connoisseurs are always interested in just how the longish pitches are struck and flighted and, for their benefit, I should perhaps add that his are mostly played with just a tinge of draw.

Seve Ballesteros, who would be the preference of many, can be almost supernatural. That last little pitch-and-run from left of the last green, when he won the 1988 Open championship at Royal Lytham and St Annes, was an unbelievable shot, remembering that it was almost impossible to be sure how the ball would come out from that lie.

Even so, I should give Langer just the edge and what may surprise a lot of folk still more is that to me that would apply additionally to the shots which have to be manufactured on account of the difficulties of lie and stance, terrain and the obstructions of nature. Seve's golfing imagination is deservedly legend but, in his own Teutonic way, Langer gets the job done time after time.

Divorcing bunker play from the other shorter shots around the green, I have to say that I rate the sand-shot as probably the

A teenage Sam Torrance, already adorned by a moustache, signs a contract to play the clubs of the world-famous John Letters company, under the eye of Jim Letters.

best in my bag. Yet the ultimate master is Gary Player who, in endless hours of practice, is said to have spent more time in sand than your average octogenarian Bedouin.

Turning to the shorter irons, I would agree that my compatriot, Bernard Gallacher, was outstanding from that range in his heyday. Gary Player may not have hit as many irons which would have had you drooling at their beauty as sundry others, but he has produced more than his quota of winners when it really mattered. But, over the seasons, I think I would go for the relentless accuracy of John Bland.

With regard to the medium irons, I reluctantly have to step outside Europe and go for a player who is more generally famed for his fairway woods – Hale Irwin, twice the US Open champion. One point, of course, is that you are probably not going to find your leading exponent of the medium irons from among the longer hitters because the number of times they use that range of club tends to be limited.

Actually, every time I start categorising iron players, I find a picture of little Guy Hunt coming back to mind for he, for no more than two seasons and perhaps for one, was the best iron player right through the bag I reckon I ever saw. However, in terms of a more lasting mastery, I should go for Nick Faldo with the long irons, save that there is only one man to whom anyone in his or her right senses could possibly hand the one-iron and that would be Sandy Lyle. Jack Nicklaus, Gary Player and many another have used a one-iron well, but Sandy Lyle with a Ping one-iron in his hand is positively awesome, indisputably one of the wonders of the golfing world.

Ian Woosnam, in full cry with victory in his sights, can hit almost any club virtually as he wants as if by instinct, but I doubt if many appreciate just how well he plays his fairway woods and, indeed, for those clubs, I can cite none better.

Just as I once headed the greens-hit-in-regulation classification on the tour, generally rated by the professionals one of the more telling statistics, so I was once voted the best driver. But I know whom I should want hitting the shot for me if I had to hand over my driver and that would be Seve Ballesteros.

I can almost see the massed raising of eyebrows in America, but forget all that stuff about Lytham 1979 and the "car-park" champion. A human howitzer like Sandy Lyle, to name but one, might be even longer off the tee when he really catches one with his driver but Seve, no matter how the golfing fraternity at large sees him, is the longest straight driver with whom I have played. Maybe he was wild in his youth before he shortened his swing preparatory to winning the 1980 US Masters, but he can be supremely good nowadays at driving for position, shaping the shot to the pattern of the hole and finding the left or right side of the fairway to ease the second. Above all, when he does miss the fairway, he usually misses it on the so-called right side.

Mind you, if you take away the factor of length, which can be so valuable an element, the accolade would have to go instead to the Merry Mex himself, Lee Trevino. He has to be the straightest driver in terms of holding fairways, with that fade of his so evident, of the last 20 years.

The ability to play in a wind is apt to be more than usually important in Britain and Ireland though, my word, make no mistake, it can blow elsewhere. John Panton was a master of flighting the ball in a crosswind but the greatest wind player has unquestionably been Christy O'Connor, senior, who would surely have started favourite in any championship played in a half gale. The way he would take a couple of clubs more than the distance suggested and hold the ball down under the wind was an object lesson to young tyros smashing the ball against the wind and hitting it so hard as to imbue it with a backspin which had it climbing fatally.

In terms of course management, of good thinking, Jack Nicklaus, with whom I was lucky enough to be paired in five rounds over consecutive Opens at Muirfield and Lytham, has been out on his own almost since his college days when he came so close to winning the US Open as an amateur.

The modern tournament professional is so much of a golfing nomad that the ability to travel well can be as valuable in itself as many of the more readily recognised golfing gifts. Nick Faldo is astonishing, capable of sandwiching a great performance in the debilitating heat of Oklahoma in the USPGA Championship tight in between being bang in contention in a Benson & Hedges international at Fulford and a Carrolls Irish Open at Portmarnock. Nevertheless, in this dimension, even Nick Faldo would have to give best to Gary Player who, a priceless

A CASE IN POINT

Suzanne and Sam with their baby, Daniel Robert. "Does he look,"
asked Bob Torrance, anxiously, in his congratulatory phone call, "an
arms-and-legs player or a hands player?"

asset in a player campaigning round the world out of Africa, can
board a plane and be fast asleep within minutes. Once he even
caused a stewardess momentary panic for, stretched out on the
floor of the plane, he was so dead to the world that she thought
he had passed away!

In my younger days, if you wanted to be among the greats of
the golfing world it was necessary to play America in no small
way. I lost a Southern Open in the United States on a play-off
and if I had won and thereby gained a three-year exemption into
their tour I might well have given it a go. As it was, I always
seemed to be too busy in Europe and elsewhere in the world and
I have to admit that I could never quite face the wrench of
deserting the European tour for the American where I would no
longer be able to get home between tournaments.

Nowadays, the rest of the golfing globe has caught up with
America – more than caught up, you may say – and I do not

myself consider that there is anything like the same call to make a prolonged attack on the US tour. Thanks to Ken Schofield, the European Tour's Executive Director, and others, the prizemoney, well over eleven million pounds in 1989, is now so big in Europe that the American purses no longer have the same attraction. Nor is that all since, apart from any other consideration, Europe offers greater variety, not least in terms of shot-making.

Since I made my debut on the tour in the early Seventies, much has improved but nothing more pertinently than the calibre of the courses we play and their conditioning, with particular reference to the fairways and the greens. The practice facilities, though better, still come in for some criticism but, though they are not as good on average as you will find in America, they are still mostly adequate. Not, I have to concede, that I am among the more habitual occupants of the practice ground; partly because, when I was a young lad, my father introduced me to the old tournament adage that "If you haven't brought it with you, you won't find it here."

Of course, if I am playing badly and my father is on hand I will work out with him at a tournament on the practice ground but, unlike so many of my brother professionals in Europe, I have not become a regular imitator of the American practice of working through several more bags of balls after a round.

That said, I cannot dispute the contention that the amount of hard work so many are now putting in is reflected in the rise of European golf vis-à-vis America and the rest of the world and, of course, in much spectacular scoring. When I first came in as a player you even then mostly had to play great golf to win, but the difference now is that the golf which would have brought you maybe sixth place in those days would be lucky to bring you 30th position now.

Another aspect of practice at tournaments is that much of it is done with in mind not so much the week in hand but the next week and the weeks beyond. Again, much depends on the individual and I am not sure that I could take, not so much

*Sam Torrance's travelling caddie, Brian Dunlop, with Bob Torrance.
The modern caddie can be much more to the itinerant tournament
professional than just the man who hefts his bag. Brian has proved a
friend and companion who, once a four-handicap golfer in his own
right and himself a native of Ayrshire, speaks the same language in
more senses than one.*

physically but mentally, the hours of unremitting practice
which a Nick Faldo can put in and apparently greatly enjoy.

On a slightly different tack, I know that much of the apparent
improvement in professional golf is ascribed by the older
brigade to advances in golfing equipment and especially in
respect of the distance the ball now travels. There is substance
in much of what they say but, perhaps because I am of a
different generation, I cannot agree with suggestions that such
innovations as square grooves and metal woods should be
outlawed.

I have a metal four-wood which I can make talk but, though I won the 1987 Italian Open using a metal-wood driver for the first two rounds, I do not think that metal-wood drivers are really for the like of me, a Seve Ballesteros or a Sandy Lyle. Not only is it much more difficult to spin the ball and work it with a metal-wood driver – I found I could cut it without too much trouble but had the devil of a job drawing it – but we hit the ball so hard as apparently to nullify the beneficial effect in terms of yardage they seem to have for some softer hitters. I have a notion, though I am not sure, that it is something to do with the way the face of a metal wood compresses at impact.

I use square grooves on my irons and I would contend that there is all the more reason to do so if, like me, you use Ping clubs because, for all the virtues of the Ping, I think a shot can more readily jump on you with them than with most other clubs if the grooves are traditional.

There are professionals who have square grooves on some of their clubs but not on others – their pitching clubs perhaps and their longest irons – but I simply cannot buy that. Let us say you have square grooves on your pitching wedge but not on your nine-iron. The gap between the two clubs, the difference, would be so pronounced as to be very disconcerting.

With me, it would always be all of them or none, and I have opted for the former because, as I see it, the advantages outweigh the disadvantages. My father begs to differ and, if it were up to him, almost all pin positions would be at the back of the green until squared grooves had been, to all intents and purposes, rendered obsolete. The player who went boldly for the flag would too often finish over the green while anyone who has square grooves appreciates how difficult it can be to pitch the ball short and let it run up to the flag.

The main disadvantages of the square grooves are firstly that, unless the shot is perfectly struck, a longish pitch-cum-approach will go nowhere into the wind and, secondly, that the deliberate flier the professionals often look to engender out of the semi-rough is close to impossible.

Sam Torrance with Gerald McKenzie, a great family friend whose brother Norman was Sam's first sponsor.

With regard to the latter, the other side of that card is that you can be in the semi-rough and still hit for the flag, confident that the shot will stop. Of course, there are those who argue that that is all wrong, that if you are in the semi-rough you should not be able to attack the flag with almost the same ease that you could from the fairway. In particular, they worry that a great links like Muirfield, which has traditionally depended on compelling the golfer to be in the right place off the tee, will lose much of its *raison d'être*.

Myself, I think they are fretting more than they need because, on an Open championship links, the square grooves could actually make such a shot from the semi-rough harder almost as often as they make it easier. Frequently on such a seaside course, you are looking to get the ball up to the flag with

39

bounce and roll but, since that is a stroke best avoided with square grooves, the alternative will be to attempt to hit a possibly much more exacting shot perfectly.

On a smaller scale, the running chip can be difficult with square grooves, though they still talk in Ayrshire of the beauty which Neil Coles conjured, admittedly from below the green, in clinching the British Seniors' Open at Turnberry in 1987. Nor is the fact that a pitch with square grooves is likely to scar a balata-covered ball to be lightly dismissed because nowadays, unless the ball is actually cut, one has to hole out with the ball with which one teed off. I know myself that when I have replaced the ball on the green with the ball markings where I like to have them, the point of the ball I want to hit is all too frequently the area roughened by the square-grooved pitch.

Nonetheless, in the final analysis, the spin you can obtain with square grooves is invaluable to the professional. With an absolutely true contact, I can get almost the same backspin with the time-honoured grooves, but with the square grooves I will still get it even with a touch of mishit. No matter which grooves are on the face of the club the first bounce will always be forward but, relatively speaking, from the standard grooves the ball will bounce, check and trickle where, from the square grooves, it will much more probably bounce, check and screw back.

The idea that square grooves are taking too much of the real art away from the game and proving too much of a leveller between the better and lesser player is again not one to which I subscribe, because the same equipment is available to everybody and skill will out.

Before leaving the matter of equipment, I have to confess that I have struck a shot or two with the various departures from the steel shaft such as graphite. I remain, though, unconvinced that for the more powerful professionals there is anything better than the steel shaft. That conviction has been reinforced by the advent of the Apollo Masterflex which gives a glorious feel and flight, the ball flying higher to a consistent length and not only

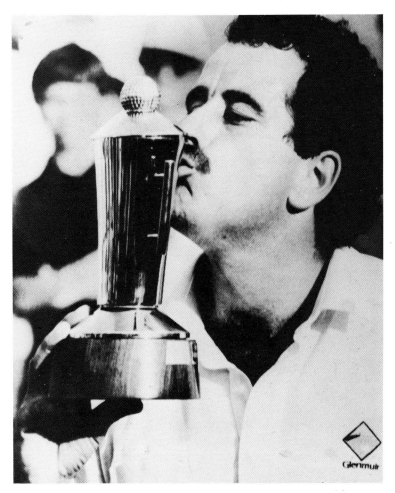

Sam Torrance kisses the trophy after winning the 1984 Benson &
Hedges International at Fulford.

with no loss of distance but, if anything, rather the reverse.

I am not such a traditionalist that I must have leather grips, but I have largish hands and prefer my grips thicker than standard. Unlike the Ben Hogans and Peter Thomsons of this world, I always favour a left-hand glove and, what is more, I keep it on even to putt. I like the feeling it gives with a putter, that sort of tightness, and have even pondered the possibility of employing a right-hand glove on the green as well.

The very first tournament I played in using those moulded, rubber-studded soles on my golf shoes I won – the 1984 Benson & Hedges International. Since then I have gone back to my previous preference for leather shoes with metal studs.

As to waterproofs, I hate having to don them, but they are often a necessity and not just in our much vilified climate. I never wear anything on my head, or very seldom, but I put on the jacket as well as the trousers, though, unless it is very cold, I will usually remove my sweater first. Incidentally, I rate myself fortunate in that neither extreme heat nor excessive cold gets to me as they do to some other players.

Now 35 – I was born on 24 August 1953 – I should still have a lot of good golf left in me in relation to the premier tours of the world. There is also the fact that the phenomenal and lucrative growth of the American Seniors' tour has prolonged the golfing ambitions of many a professional and is having a spin-off in other countries. Gary Player, a fitness fanatic, has already done the Grand Slam of Seniors' golf – though not in the one year – and has announced his intention of still playing golf of the front rank when he has turned 60.

I have never been persuaded of the need to train specifically, partly because I was lucky enough to be naturally strong and long. But I do have one very great regret and that is that I did not look after my body better in my earlier years in the matter of eating the right things. I stand five feet eleven inches which some deem almost the ideal height for a golfer, but my weight once went up to fifteen and a half stones. Whereupon I dieted down to ten and a half stones and predictably, as I now realise, lost my game and my swing. Now I am something over thirteen stone. This is my optimum weight but the reason I feel like a new man in my mid-thirties is that I am now on a diet, "Fit for Life". By definition, a tournament professional's life is one course after another but not, if you are wise, in the culinary sense.

THREE

DESPITE OR BECAUSE?

Bobby Jones, Ben Hogan and Jack Nicklaus would figure prominently in any poll on the three greatest players of all time and yet, in many ways, in terms of swing and technique they were worlds apart. Changes in conditions and equipment over the years obviously come into it and certainly there are points in common, not least, as with any good player, at impact. But the point I would make is that when three such players are so different, any suggestion that there is only one correct way to play golf is plainly nonsense.

Most teachers claim to teach not so much a method as the man or woman, but all of us, myself included, have our own pet convictions. Even so, I think that though the swing has obviously evolved over the years, most of the best instruction is still based on time-honoured golfing truths and that much else proves to be no more than a passing vogue.

For instance, the cult of square to square may have helped some but many of its disciples now think of it merely as a fad which came and went. Certainly, the notion that its advent was tantamount to the day of golfing revelation has not stood the test of time. Many of the accepted golf commandments – such, for instance, as a straight left arm or a still head – have been broken by champions and yet those very commandments may be integral to the success of another household name's game.

Nowadays I am coach to Scotland's national amateur squad and I have to ask myself whether, if a Bobby Locke, with his

43

closed stance and habitual draw, or a Lee Trevino, with his
open stance and staple fade, had come to me before they had
made their reputations, I would have had the good sense to
leave well alone or, at any rate, build on what they had. Of
course, I like to think I would but . . ..

Some years ago, Deane Beman, whom I have come to know
in his capacity as the American Tour Commissioner but who
won the Amateur championships on both sides of the Atlantic,
wrote a brilliant series in which he noted points of technique
which, as he put it succinctly but memorably, were mutually
exclusive.

Not just the tutor but the taught have to know what goes with
what in their understanding of the swing, while always for the
great coach the trick is to decide whether, in the case of a player
with something unorthodox or unconventional in his swing, he
is successful despite it or because of it.

FOUR

THE GRIP

Basically, there are three grips in the sense of the overlapping grip which was, as far as we know, invented by The Honourable Company's J. E. Laidlay, but popularised by Harry Vardon; the interlocking grip which is chiefly, but not exclusively, favoured by those with small hands such as Gene Sarazen and Jack Nicklaus; and the two-handed or baseball grip which was utilised by another golfer with smallish paws in the person of Dai Rees and by a player such as the famed Scottish amateur, Jack McLean, when he was experimenting in a search for greater length. There have even been those who switched between the two, the happiest example perhaps being Julius Boros who won the 1952 US Open interlocking and the 1963 US Open overlapping.

In the end, it comes down, to no small extent, to what feels most comfortable, though if, for instance, you decide to experiment with an interlocking grip, having previously overlapped, it is only sensible to give yourself time to grow accustomed to the change and rid yourself of the frequently experienced feeling of awkwardness born out of unfamiliarity.

That the importance of the grip can scarcely be exaggerated should not be interpreted as an assertion that there is only one true grip. Gene Sarazen, who won championships with a grip which showed four knuckles to a degree which shook the purists and in which his left thumb hung loose off the grip outside the

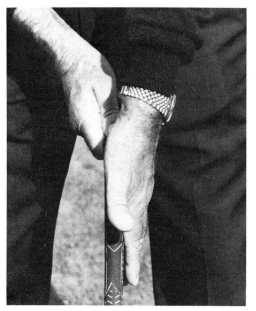

Fitting the left hand

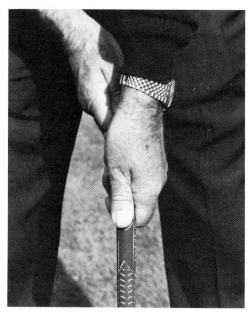

Left hand closes on grip

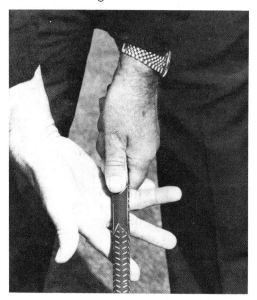

Fitting the right hand

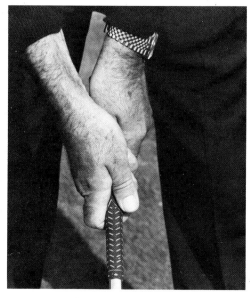

The completed grip

THE GRIP

A sound grip will harmonise with a good set-up. The foundation has been laid for the left hand to play its part in providing the outline of the swing and in taking the additional explosiveness of the hit at impact provided, preferably instinctively rather than by a conscious application, by the right hand. As for the right hand itself, if the grip is right, not only will the right hand fulfil its natural role of helping to squaare the clubface up at impact but it will have been that much easier for the right elbow to have folded correctly on the backswing.

right hand – "the most contorted bunch of bananas I have ever seen", said one pundit – declared on the eve of the 1988 US Masters that the great difference between him and Bobby Jones was that Jones had a beautiful grip from the first while he had to find one he could make work for him. He also believes that much more than an advance in golf clubs, improved gripping of the club by the players, together with the advance in golf-ball manufacture and the fact that mankind generally is bigger, explains any improvement which has taken place over the years and nowhere more spectacularly than in terms of length.

Tommy Armour, who was said to use his hands on a golf club like Kreisler fiddling on a Stradivarius, once remarked that all experts kept uncovering something fresh about the grip: "In fifteen years," he wrote in 1967, "our youngsters, both girls and boys, will be so far ahead of us that we won't be able to imagine that they are the same sort of creatures." Great judge of distance though Armour was, at least before he lost an eye in the Kaiser's War, he would have been guilty of under-clubbing more times

| *My preferred left-hand finger and palm grip* | *To me, this left-hand grip is too much in the fingers* |

than he ever was of understatement but the point he makes is valid.

To an extent, physique may dictate the grip, it being one of Henry Cotton's contentions that the short, thick-necked, barrel-chested golfer could not play with his elbows close together and therefore had to be prepared to show three or four knuckles on the left hand. The American professional, Porky Oliver, who gave the impression of coming in to the ball with the side of his left hand leading, did nothing to refute that opinion but, as always, there are plenty of exceptions, while Bobby Locke thickened with the years without changing from the relatively "weak" grip of his slim youth.

One of the accepted tenets has been that in a good grip the Vs formed by the thumb and forefinger on the two hands will not oppose but will point very much in the same direction: to the right shoulder where more knuckle on the left hand is shown and virtually to the chin in the case of, say, Henry Cotton's much-copied two-knuckle grip. But, once more, it is wrong to be too dogmatic, because Tony Lema played glorious golf with a powerful grip in which the V of the right hand was well outside that of the left.

THE GRIP

In terms of what should be the pressure points in the grip, there has been a shift of view down the decades, with Vardon emphasising the grip of the forefingers and thumbs and Tommy Armour selling countless books on the score of the right-hand lash he held emanated from the trigger grip of the right forefinger.

For my own part, I side with those who emphasise the firm hold throughout the swing of the last three fingers of the left hand – something which Armour, incidentally, similarly stressed – and of the middle two fingers of the right hand. Ben Hogan suggested that the right feeling was induced by practising with both the right thumb and the right forefinger off the club. I should endorse that because, where Armour speaks of the right forefinger and the thumb in terms of power, I think of that combination more in the light of sensitivity and touch.

Two other points with regard to the grip are all too often overlooked but should be borne in mind by the more ambitious pupil. Firstly, how many knuckles a player will appear to show can depend on whether he has his hands forward in the so-called K address with the left arm and club shaft in virtually a straight line, or relatively far back in the address. Secondly, there are finger grippers and palm grippers and those who are something of both. Hogan and Trevino, to name but two, would go down in my book as palm grippers, but Cotton and Snead as finger grippers. The contrast between the two is the extent to which the club lies in the left hand along the roots of the fingers or more obliquely across the palm and, though even this is only a generalisation, the finger grippers tend to be hands players and the palm grippers to set more store on body action and the use of the legs.

Though there is no one correct grip for all and sundry that does not preclude each player finding what is the optimum grip for him or her. As a teacher, I am always prepared to tolerate variations and even to experiment a little with the individual pupil. In the vast majority of cases, the best grip is also the most conventional in terms of a matching of the Vs and nothing too

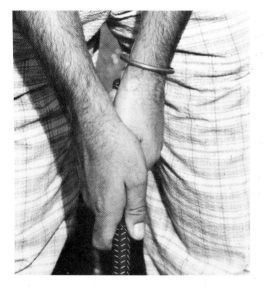

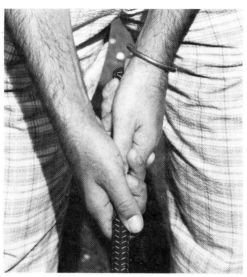

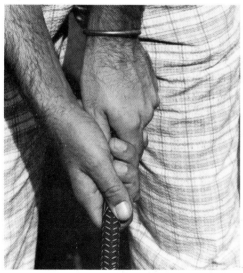

Above left, the slicer's grip, right hand a little too far over on top of the club and a very "weak" left hand with the V pointing to the left eye.

Above right, the most feeble grip in the game with the Vs not married but opposed.

Left, the hooker's grip with the left hand showing all four knuckles and the right hand dangerously under. Yet it is worth remembering that many a golfer with variations of such a grip ends up actually moving the ball left to right as he blocks out the hook.

extreme in terms of a "strong" or "weak" hold on the club, strong being the golfing term used to describe a grip in which something not too far short of the maximum amount of knuckle is shown on the left hand and weak a one-knuckle or, just possibly, two-knuckle grip.

Harold Hilton, 'way back before the turn of the century, allowed the club at the top of the backswing to drop down into the V of the right hand and yet, in an enviable record, was his achievement in becoming at Muirfield in 1892 both the first amateur and the first Englishman to win the Open. Henry Cotton always added Neil Coles and Peter Thomson to the accepted example of Dai Rees with regard to a certain slipping of the right hand in the course of the backswing but, as Coles always emphasises, certain liberties may perhaps be taken with the right hand but the grip with the left hand should remain snug and firm from first to last.

Even among the more famous, many a golfer has suffered from a tendency for his hands to come apart at the top. Tommy Armour was always held to be, in the phrase of the day, the glass of fashion where hand action was concerned, but he went through a miserable spell until Claude Harmonn verged on the heretical by suggesting, rightly as it happened, that Armour's hands were coming apart. My own son, Sam, has had the same problem and, frequently, I have had him hitting shots either with a blade of grass or, better still, because you can feel it more readily, a coin lodged between the left thumb and the butt of the right hand.

I am often asked by women if I consider, as so many have down the years, that they should adopt a somewhat "strong" grip in search of the right to left flight which will help to compensate for a lack of masculine strength. My stance on that issue is that, partly through the growth of the professional game on the distaff side in Europe now as well as in America, women's golf is greatly improving overall and, as it does so, gets rather closer to the men's game in most respects and not least in this matter of the grip.

I am on the side of the traditionalists in that I still see the left hand as the controlling hand and the right hand as the hitting hand or, as some put it, in what can be a rather dangerous image, the throwing hand. Nevertheless, I have reservations for the ordinary player concerning the practice of such revered swingers as Bobby Jones and Tommy Armour who made something of a fetish of a very light grip with the right hand.

Actually, on the subject of lightness of grip, there have been players who found helpful such similes as holding the club as gently as you would a bird or with no more than the squeeze you would give a full tube of toothpaste, but I reckon that even though the left hand may be the dominant in terms of providing the outline of the swing, a grip that is nice and firm without being strained or white-knuckled is right for both hands.

The right-hand grip, I repeat, should always be in the fingers with the palm grippers confining that preference to the left hand, where the player also has a choice of a long left thumb or a short one. That in itself is worth some experiment to find out what suits the individual, for switching to a short left thumb curtailed Ben Hogan's tendency toward a perhaps dangerously long backswing and was a feature of the change of swing which led to his greatest triumphs. As always, much will depend on a player's physical characteristics, the shape and possibly the size of his hands and also their flexibility.

In the last resort – and it is the main reason, of course, for overlapping and interlocking – the most vital thing is that the hands should work together in perfect unison. Here, too, there is more licence than many might suppose for there have been outstanding performers whose hand action in the all-important hitting area confounded personal idiosyncrasies.

FIVE

THE STANCE

The placement of the feet in the stance has evolved to the point where such golfing immortals as Ben Hogan and Jack Nicklaus stand with their right foot at virtually 90 degrees to the line of play and their left foot turned out somewhere between 30 degrees and 45 degrees. That is the placement I endorse but it would be idiotic to suggest that those players of yesteryear, or of today, who would not conform to those angles of foot placement, were wrong.

That grand all-round games player, W. W. Lowe, in his book, *Bedrock Principles of Golf*, published no longer ago than 1937, actually advocated a stance which was almost a direct contradiction of that adopted by the like of Hogan and Nicklaus, Lowe having the left foot at right angles to the line of play on the grounds that if it were turned outwards it hampered the backswing. Most of the celebrated players of bygone years were less extreme than Lowe but Tommy Armour, who won the Open championships of both the Old World and the New, had his right foot turned out, particularly with the woods where his stance was notably closed. Sam Snead had his right foot turned out, though not as much as the left, while among the moderns it is worth noting that Tom Watson's right foot is turned out to some 20 degrees.

I have always thought that feet turned outwards to exactly the same extent conveyed the impression of a vague stance, the opposite of businesslike in that you would not know simply from looking at the feet in which direction the player was playing. Of course, the set of the feet in respect of how you walk comes into it. It was no coincidence that Cotton, naturally somewhat pigeon-toed, mirrored that characteristic in his stance, albeit as a hands player who markedly hit past the chin he had less reason to open up the left foot than an arms and legs player.

Minor adjustments of the angle of the feet can make a considerable difference to the feel of the swing. Leonard Crawley, a born hitter of almost any kind of ball but a noted theorist and good teacher into the bargain, once put the stocky little Welsh bulldog, Brian Huggett, back on the right track simply by persuading him to turn his right foot out a little, which allowed him to clear his right hip on the backswing more easily. Indeed, many of the more heavily built who are not exactly svelte around the hips may find that a very valuable tip though, heaven knows, you could not get anyone much more heavily built than Jack Nicklaus when he first burst upon the golfing world, and his stance was basically the same then as it is today.

What I particularly like about a stance in which the right foot is at right angles to the line of play and the left foot turned outwards is that such an angle of the right foot encourages the resistance you must get from a flexed right knee as you swing back and the drive or kick off it which ideally you want in the downswing. I do not say for a moment that there is no resistance with the right foot turned outward, but it is less part and parcel of the set-up and probably explains to my mind why the players of yesteryear swung back against the straight right leg which is somewhat frowned upon nowadays.

Pupils have to be treated as individuals but I incline towards a stance which is on the wide side rather than the narrow. In my own case, for a five-iron, lines down from my shoulders would be level with the inside of my heels. Patently, it narrows a little with the shorter clubs and *vice versa* with the longer.

I like a feeling of springiness, of being alive on the balls of the feet with the weight, aside from how else it is distributed, inclining towards the inside of the feet.

Sam Torrance plays a shot left-handed with his sand-wedge reversed.

Driver address   *Five-iron address*

THE ADDRESS

In my teaching philosophy, the same swing applies to all standard shots right down through the bag, the only changes being those brought about by the length and lie of the particular club in hand.

Points to note are the stance with the right foot, as I like to see it, either at right angles to the line of play or, as in my case, slightly turned out. The left foot has to be turned out somewhere between 30 degrees and 45 degrees, unless you are as pigeon-toed as was Henry Cotton. In other words, the natural set of the feet and how, consequently, you walk, can provide a guide for teacher and pupil.

Pitching-wedge address

For all full shots, I argue for an equal distribution of the weight. There have, though, been great golfers who liked the feeling of having more weight on the right foot at the driver address when the ball has to be swept into the great beyond and players who favoured setting up for everything, save possibly the drive, with the weight a little on the left side and all the more so as they got closer to the green and the length of shot shortened.

A desirable address has many connotations but in golf it asks for a straight back with the head nicely up, the posterior out and the knees flexed. Build will dictate to some extent but ideally the elbows should be together. The hands should be snugly wed and the Vs also married.

Driver address

Five-iron

Pitching-wedge

The stance, set-up and posture represented in these pictures are within the reach of even the most untalented and yet, get all that correct and you are already a long way towards hitting a very respectable golf shot.

Sam Torrance at the address with an iron. Note the comfortable set-up and stance, with the head behind the ball and the relation of the hands to the ball, which is itself located inside the left heel.

SIX

SET-UP

The first thing to understand about the set-up, and just about the most neglected among those who in clubhouse discussions pay it lip service, is that the player does not set up to the ball and then ground the club but sets the face of the club to the ball and then sets himself to the club.

There are various ways of moving into the address position and those who think that standing initially with the feet together prior to spreading them into the stance is a latter-day innovation may like to know that Tommy Armour moved into his address position in precisely that manner.

Some move into their address or set-up with, to begin with, just the right hand on the club or only the left, and they should be aware of the effect that can have on squaring up the shot on the lines they want. If, like Bernhard Langer, you shape to the shot with only the right hand on the club then, when you add the left, you will find that actually helps to square the shoulders and the top half of your body to the intended line. If, in contrast, you move into the address with just the left hand on the club, as did Frank Stranahan and as does Greg Norman, you will have to fight a tendency, when you add the right, for the right shoulder to come forward, leaving the upper half of the body more open than was intended.

Incidentally, in the matter of moving into the address with just the one hand on the club, Greg Norman ran into an interesting problem on the evening of the third day of his victory in the 1986 Open championship at Turnberry. Into the storm of wind and rain, he found that by the time he applied the second hand to the club, both it and the relevant part of the grip were soaking and so he did the very difficult thing of departing from his habitual ritual and settling to the shot with both hands on the club.

Reverting to the shoulders, many a player has slipped without knowing it into the bad practice of aiming his shoulders at the flag whereas the right picture is of a railway track in which the player is on one rail and the clubface and ball on the other. In other words, the shoulders, following the track, should be aimed that amount left of the target.

Australia's Peter Thomson, the quintuple Open champion, is generally credited with being the first great golfer who tended to talk in terms of set-up rather than the address position. The phrase may not have been his originally but the point is that it was so useful in getting across the right image that it has stuck.

Thomson himself was an apostle of a set-up wherein virtually a straight line ran down from the left shoulder through the left arm to the shaft of the club, and he paid careful attention to what he termed "measuring off" with regard to distance from the ball. But, as always, there is no one way which is right for everybody.

Bobby Jones noted that slow-motion films revealed that, whereas at impact his hands were slightly in front of the ball, Harry Vardon's were fractionally behind it. It was, as Jones added, reflected in their address positions and, more and more, the theory has been that the set-up or position at address should come as close as is compatible with comfort and balance to duplicating the position at impact.

Jack Nicklaus, like Thomson, sets up in what has come to be known as the K position, with left arm and club forming something close to a straight line, but others have favoured something more akin to a Y in the triangle formed by their arms and the club. Billy Casper and Ben Hogan, to cite but two, had their hands farther back at the address than many purists would have recommended, while the Scottish professional, North Berwick's David Huish, had an especially interesting case history. Always more of a club professional than a tournament player, Huish was nevertheless good enough to lead the Open Championship at Carnoustie in 1975 at the halfway stage. Few could believe that such a skilled and seasoned golfer, with no small reputation as a teacher himself, could play with his hands so far back, but the fact of the matter was that when Huish attempted to make the conventional change on the urging of his famed compatriot, Eric Brown, he could not, as they say, hit his hat.

As an instructor, I seek to foster an address position which inclines towards the K without anything too rigid in the way of that straight line down through the left arm and club. That also encourages a comparatively high left shoulder which, provided it is not exaggerated, mirrors the position at impact and serves to invest the left side, arm and hand with the sensation of dominance which I consider they should have. What is more, that kind of thinking has stood the test of time, for James Braid, of the "Great Triumvirate", was wont to take a new assistant out on to the course at Walton Heath and make him set up to the ball on the steep upslope of a bunker face. "That," he used to say, "is the feeling I want you to have in future when you address a golf-ball."

Many teachers stress the importance of setting up square, and certainly that has its advantages when it comes to starting a beginner. But, as the pupil advances, he or she should come to understand that the saying that the straight shot, the ball hit without any kind of side-spin, is the hardest and most elusive in golf is no empty cliché. Most of the better players, not just on the professional scene but even in the upper strata of the amateur game, are looking to work the ball one way or the other, and that holds even more true today than it once did because of the adoption in these islands of the 1.68 or larger ball.

Jack Nicklaus sets up slightly open; Seve Ballesteros, at least in my experience, quite a bit closed, at any rate from the tee.

The important thing to me is not whether you prefer to fade the ball from an open stance or draw it from a closed one, but that everything marries in the sense, particularly, of the shoulders and feet.

I know that there have been teachers who have had success with the higher handicap players in having them set up with the shoulders a little closed and the hips open in order to help their turn on the backswing and their clearance on the downswing, but that way is not my way.

With regard to weight distribution, the teachers of earlier days asserted that because you are going to hit the drive on the up – or, more accurately, have the feeling of doing so – 60 per cent of the weight should be on the right foot at the driver address. By the same token, they preached that the weight should be progressively more on the left side the closer you got to the green and should mostly stay there throughout the swing for a short iron or wedge. Possibly the equipment, in terms of the clubs and balls with which they played, had something to do with it, though as shrewd a swing analyst as Cary Middlecoff stated recently that not only did he himself have 60 per cent of the weight on the right foot in his driver address but so, too, did many of the leading golfers of today.

I would myself go along with Nicklaus' thinking, which in turn followed that of Bobby Jones, and have the weight evenly distributed, save for specific out-of-the-ordinary shots or actual pitches and chips.

Again, I have no quarrel with those who open up the stance to facilitate the clearance of the left hip and let the club more readily go through towards the flag as they move down to the shorter irons. Yet, I have never seen any reason why the stance, though it may narrow, should change greatly, if at all, in terms of the alignment and set of the feet from the driver down to the wedges. All of which ties in with my conception that set-up and swing are fundamentally the same right through the bag.

Consistent with that line of thinking is my belief that, for all normal shots, the ball position remains the same, a few swings being enough to determine where the low point of a particular player's swing lies. Bobby Jones, Ben Hogan and Jack Nicklaus all adhere to that principle and so does my own offspring, Sam, but there have been plenty of superb strikers who did not.

Most of the golfers of earlier times moved the ball back in the stance as the clubs shortened and the loft increased until they were pitching with the ball off the right foot. Sam Snead, whose tournament days span more than half a century from the Twenties, adheres to the same maxim without bringing the ball quite so far back, while a player like Tom Watson also brings it back as he goes down through his quiver of clubs, though seldom does he have it right of centre even with a wedge other than for a "type" shot.

Seve Ballesteros, who, as a small boy, learned to play with just the one club, a three-iron, and who, perhaps as a legacy, has always been prepared to work things out for himself, reckons that there is more logic on the side of those who are prepared to bring the ball back in the stance as the length and loft of the club changes. After all, he reasons, using the extreme, the angle of the attack is hardly the same when you are sweeping a driver away off a peg-tee into the far distance as it is when you are taking a divot with your wedge.

Like so much else in golf, it is for the player, in conjunction with his coach, to find out which theory in the matter of ball positioning works best for him or her. But, as I say, without being blinkered on the subject, I like to number the ball position among the constants of the swing except when stance or lie, the shape of the hole or the wind, or a combination of those factors, asks for something very different from the standard shot.

Bob Torrance keeping a helpful eye on Sandy Lyle (on right) at the 1983 Ryder Cup in America at Palm Beach. Sandy Lyle's swing is still basically the one his father, Alex Lyle, the Hawkstone Park professional, fostered in him from infancy but, in terms of a swing service when away on tour, Alex Lyle has never had any objection to his son seeking the advice of such leading professionals as Scotland's Bob Torrance and America's Jim Ballard.

SEVEN

PRE-SHOT ROUTINE, WAGGLE AND FORWARD PRESS

Bert Yancey, in the days when he came to Britain to play in the Open, used to speak of "that awful moment when you have to take the club back . . .". He was speaking humorously, of course, but the very fact that so many golfers know at once what he meant in itself underlines the importance of the pre-shot routine, waggle and forward press, even if it is possible to point to great players who seemed to have little or no need of all three.

Gene Sarazen, for instance, at one time in his career seemed to settle into almost every shot differently and yet unloose a stream of winners. Seve Ballesteros has often struck me as virtually doing without a waggle. Again, there are golfers whose forward press is either almost invisible, such as the firming-up of the grip with which at one time Jack Nicklaus used to trigger his swing, or whose last waggle does duty as a form of forward press.

Routine or ritual can be very important from tee to green. Billy Casper, if something interrupted his habitual pre-shot preparation, would actually go so far as to stick the club back in the bag and begin again. Bobby Jones always said that the moment he took an extra waggle he could look for trouble, while Bobby Locke always took the same two practice swings before setting about holing a putt.

There are no hard-and-fast rules, but the great thing is to train yourself to do the same thing each time so as to establish an overall rhythm, one advantage being that you will not get fatally

Seve Ballesteros with Bob Torrance at the 1983 Masters at Augusta. Seve believes that his right hand and right side control his swing whereas Bob maintains that for the great majority of golfers the left side has to provide the dominant guideline. But the two enjoy discussing techniques and mostly see eye to eye.

stuck over a difficult shot or one which has come to matter an awful lot more than most because of the cumulative pressure.

The waggle can be of great assistance in freeing the golfer from too much tension and helping him settle into a shot, but it can become a disease. Indeed, everyone in golf is familiar with the story of how Tommy Armour was told by his caddie to aim on a distant post but, when he finally brought himself to play the shot, struck it straight as an arrow into a bunker. He rounded on his caddie but saw the funny side when he realised that the post in question was the mast of a ship which by then had put out to sea.

Sam Snead has a lovely waggle and, personally, I do not think it matters a great deal whether the waggle takes place, as with so many of the moderns, behind the ball or over it. It is a matter of personal preference but I have seen golfers spoil the

Bob Torrance driving in the course of a game with his favourite fourball. David Gemmell is on the left, Jim McAllister to his right, with Matt McCrorie almost wholly obscured between them.

ease of their pre-shot process by making the waggle too artificial.

In fact, Ben Hogan, though he attached great importance to certain aspects of the waggle, such as the right elbow touching the right hip, argued against grooving the waggle. As he so often recalled, he had learned from watching that short-game magician, John Revolta, whose waggle, in Herb Warren Wind's famous phrase, was a kind of trailer for the coming attraction. In other words Hogan, like Revolta, used the waggle as a rehearsal for the stroke to come, slow and soft if that was appropriate to the shot ahead, or brisk and staccato if that was the kind of impact to be desired.

One of the benefits of a waggle is that it helps the golfer to stay in motion, keep alive. Doug Sanders had really no waggle as such but, if you watched closely, his feet were constantly shifting a little right up to the moment when he swung the club away. Again, the Ryder Cup player, England's Paul Way, hit a terrible slump which ended, temporarily at least, when he forced himself to waggle and blend from it straight into the shot, his reward being the 1987 European Open at Walton Heath.

The forward press takes many forms and, in the course of a career, even the best players sometimes change that little something which detonates their swing. Jack Nicklaus, by way of a prelude to his swing, for long merely firmed up his grip and turned his head away to the right, pre-setting it where such as Sam Snead let it turn with the backswing. Latterly, a slight and gentle rocking of the body to the left has been discernible as Nicklaus is about to pull the trigger.

The forward press is more vital to some than to others, though even those who are less conscious of it probably have some movement prior to takeaway which they could not do without even if they tried. Cary Middlecoff, the former US Open champion, used to complain that one of the problems he had with bunker play was that the rule forbidding the touching of the sand before the swing cut out the forward press which was so much a part of his overall tempo and rhythm.

Talk golf to Sam Snead and he will tell you that he never hit a shot in his life which did not begin with a forward press, his own version being a classic but by no means exaggerated pressing down of the club with the hands and a little kick in with the right knee.

But the aspect of the forward press which I should always want to emphasise is that it can take many forms, an obvious example being the way Billy Casper regrips with his right foot immediately before moving into the backswing.

In summation, I like my pupils to acquire a simple but standard pre-shot routine, a waggle that is not necessarily much more than a means of getting the feel of the club and the shot in mind, and a forward press which will do much to avoid a "dead" swing. Yet, as in so many other areas of the swing, one has grown wary of dogmatism. To cite but one obvious case, the old teachers used to say that there was nothing worse than to waggle suitably, then set the club behind the ball and, instead of going straight into the swing, with or without the aid of a forward press, let everything go dead again. But isn't that just what Jack Nicklaus so often seems to do before his own interpretation of the forward press sets one of the great actions of all time in motion?

EIGHT

TAKEAWAY AND ARM ROTATION

The so-called one-piece takeaway may represent the orthodox but different golfers favour different emphasis and, even in the same player, it does not necessarily stay constant. Julius Boros, a formidable enough player to win the US Open twice, had at one time the belief that if he got his left shoulder turning the rest of the backswing would more or less take care of itself. Yet he came later to feel that the backswing was best sensed in the hands and that if they moved correctly along the right path all would be well.

There are golfers, like Joyce Wethered, who believed in a one-piece takeaway, but one dictated by the hands, and others who placed their faith in a hands-and-arm takeaway or in a takeaway controlled by the left hand and arm.

Still others preferred to think of the whole of the left side beginning the backswing, while a rival school might arrive at a not dissimilar top-of-the-backswing position by focusing on clearing the right hip on the backswing or, alternatively or simultaneously, turning the right shoulder back and out of the way.

Similarly, there have always been golfers who favoured in hands first in the takeaway and others who did better with the clubhead leading the hands even if they stopped short of the early set which was associated with Johnny Miller and, for a period, with the square to square theory.

71

Though there are unorthodox swings which prove the exception, sound left-arm rotation is a feature of most good swings. If you do not already have it, the chances are that you will be a very much better golfer for acquiring it. It allows, consistent with a quiet and steady head, the widest possible backswing in which the right elbow will not fly. Above all, nothing so helps the player to put the club "in the slot" at the top time after time.

Many players make the dire mistake of confusing the rotation of the left arm with a rolling of the wrists.

Some very great players, including Bobby Jones and Bobby Locke, have been across the line at the top but not, as here, high and awkwardly because of a failure to rotate the left arm to the requisite degree.

If it were not a five-iron which was being used, but the longer swing of a driver, the backswing would have continued to the point where the club was on line to the target.

73

The hands leading into the backswing, which produced that touch of drag which was held to be good form in the days of such as Harry Vardon, Bobby Jones and even Henry Cotton, was a product of the hickory shaft and, to an extent, the small ball. There was an element of what I would term flick in the relatively pronounced hand action they sought through impact. It is different for the modern golfer and, though there is nothing wrong with a one-piece takeaway, I should always prefer that, if anything, the clubhead led into the backswing. To me, and it is one of the planks of my teaching, the clubhead going away first blends with the correct clockwise rotation of the left arm. If they are wed then it is not too difficult to arrive at the same position at the top of the backswing time after time.

The aforesaid rotation of the left arm may happen without the player thinking about it, but if it does not then he has to learn it because, make no mistake, it is a desirable ingredient of a correct and power-laden backswing. Many, indeed, have come to the conclusion that its rotation going back and the reciprocal rotation on the return into impact are important factors in providing clubhead speed and length.

Two points should perhaps be noted. First, the player with a strong grip and a lot of knuckles showing on the left hand will rotate less because his grip ensures that he is already part of the way there. Second, and very important, the rotation takes place in the forearm and is certainly not to be confused with that fatal rolling of the wrists on the backswing.

There are players who, because of the nature of their backswings, rotate less than others, Miller Barber being one who springs readily to my mind. A player with an orthodox grip who yet shuts the club at the top of the backswing and, accordingly, plays from shut to open, will clearly have less rotation. Yet it can be a supreme element in a golfer's swing and had much to do with Ben Hogan's superb striking in the later years of his tournament career.

As to the track on which the clubhead should go back, that, too, can vary from player to player. A man like the late Tony

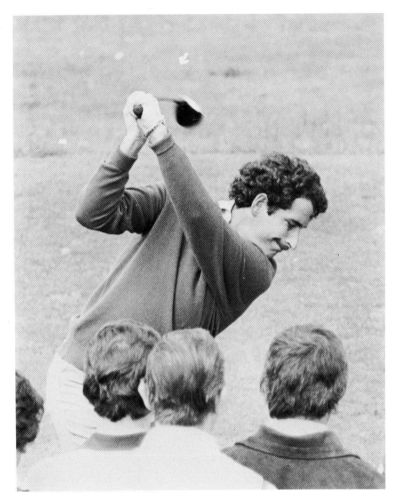

Sam Torrance in the slot at the top, with the left wrist square.

Lema, who looped to the inside, frequently gave the impression that he had taken the club back slightly outside the line. Yet another with his name on our Open Championship trophy, Sandy Lyle, brings it inside on the backswing quite sharply.

The great English amateur, Ronnie White, always stressed that if the club-face were still square to the line of flight after six inches the player was more than halfway towards a straight shot, but my own teaching is that the correct takeaway will move inside with the natural turn of the shoulders and body which, for its part, will have been founded on the right footwork.

There are golfers such as Jack Nicklaus, my own son, Sam, and that outstanding English amateur, Michael Bonallack, who have played without grounding the club at address. Apart from the fact that it removed any danger of the club catching on any little obstruction on the takeaway, they liked the feeling it promoted at the start of the backswing. In contrast, Seve Ballesteros tried it and found that it was not for him, that it made him snatch. It also, of course, can complicate a player's long-established form of forward press. I do not condemn it but I do not teach it either.

Ballesteros has revealed how his own sensation is that of swinging the club away into the backswing with his right hand while Ben Hogan once advised Cary Middlecoff – though you won't find it anywhere in Hogan's writings – to take the club back with the right and hit with the left. The very antithesis of what Tommy Armour and company taught.

As so often in the swing, each player has to be treated as an individual in the matter of starting the takeaway, the art of the matter being to find out what feeling and/or picture works best for the pupil in question. Fundamentally, though, I like the left side in general and the left arm and hand in particular to be in control in the sense of providing the outline of the swing, but I should never want the right hand in the grip to be so subservient and lax as to be in danger of coming back into the action just too suddenly and convulsively.

Never lose sight of the fact that golf is a game of two hands and that, for the best results, they must work together in blessed union.

A majestic swing in a fitting setting. Sam Torrance in Switzerland, at the top of the swing, club beautifully on line.

Sam Torrance playing in the 1982 Spanish Open at Club de Campo, Madrid. Right knee flexed, right elbow pointing down, club on line to the target.

NINE

WEIGHT SHIFT ON THE BACKSWING

Let me concede right away that even among the acknowledged luminaries of golf instruction there is apt to be a divergence of opinion on the degree of transference of weight which takes place in the course of a good golf swing. Just what a minefield this area can be may be readily gauged from the fact that probably no one, before or since, has written better on the golf swing than Bobby Jones, and yet even he appears at times to contradict himself. For instance: "It is," wrote Jones, "my definite opinion that there need be no shifting of weight from left foot to right during the backstroke. I have examined numbers of photographs of the very best players and I have been able to find no case in which a shifting was perceptible." But again, from the same pen: "It is necessary in order to swing easily and rhythmically that there be an appreciable shift of weight successively backward to the right foot in taking the club back, and forward to the left in striking the ball."

Bobby Jones played all his standard shots right through the bag with the ball off the left heel and so, since he was already behind the ball, presumably felt less need than most to move the weight back. Yet, for myself, when I see how high his left heel came off the ground in the backswing, and for all that no doubt there was still some weighty pressure exerted on the ground from the vicinity of his left toe, I cannot believe that his weight did not shift a deal more on the backswing than he himself supposed.

The left knee has shot forward, failing to come in pointing behind the ball as it should on the backswing. As an inevitable consequence, the right hip has failed to clear and any chance of a correct weight shift has been destroyed.

The left knee, with the push coming from the vicinity of the left toe, is pointing in behind the ball with the right hip cleared. Such old-timers as James Braid, who pushed off the inside of the left foot from the toe back to the arch, had the knee pointing in more laterally and so, too, though not quite to the same degree, does a player like Nicklaus whose heavy build necessitates a relatively full hip turn and who learned his footwork by rolling over on the insides of his feet. Note that the left heel should not be consciously lifted but can legitimately be pulled up in the course of the swing, much depending on the player in question's physique. But even those who keep the left foot planted still get plenty of foot action with the inward roll from the left ankle.

One of Bob Torrance's favourite pictures. Jack Nicklaus at the top of the backswing with, partly because of his build, his left heel pulled well off the turf in a superb weight transference, the right hip fully cleared, the shoulder turn 90 degrees or more and the club on line. A more ample and powerful coil it would be difficult to envisage.

Various machines have been made which purport to measure the distribution of weight between the two feet at address, at the top of the backswing, at impact and in the follow-through but, whatever they may be held to prove, I do not personally believe they are all that relevant because it is what the golfer feels which matters.

I encourage my pupils to have the sensation of having somewhere around 80 per cent of their weight on the right foot at the top of the backswing, though I would never deny that such a weight shift is much more apparent in a player like Roberto de Vicenzo than in many another.

The twin keys, in my book, to achieving such a weight shift lie in getting the left knee pointing in behind the ball and clearing the right hip. A golfer may think of either or both, there being no objection to the latter since the two go together as Siamese twins. I know, before the reader raises the objection, that such as Ben Hogan have talked about restricting the hip turn, but the degree to which he did that was only relative.

In making such a weight shift on the backswing, the resistance, which stops you from overdoing it, comes nowadays from the flexed right knee where golfers of bygone days more often obtained it from the straightening of the right leg. Mark you, Lee Trevino seems to me to straighten his right leg no less than did such players of yesteryear as Bobby Jones, Tommy Armour, Henry Cotton and Bobby Locke. It is worth mentioning, while on the subject, that the young Henry Cotton noted that he seemed to play his best golf when he did not allow his right leg to become just too stiff and straight. Armour always spoke of the need for an easy looseness right up to the right hip spreading from the address into the action of the feet and hips.

Though James Braid had his left knee going across much more than most on the backswing, I prefer the angle of the left knee to be more oblique. But overdoing the inward shift is arguably a much lesser fault than allowing the left knee to droop forward rather than going across to point in behind the ball because, aside from the harm that does to the weight shift, it does nothing to encourage the clearing of the right hip.

The young Jack Nicklaus was encouraged by his legendary mentor, Jack Grout, to keep both heels on the ground and roll from the ankles in order to build the footwork Grout wanted. There is certainly nothing wrong with that in itself and the Nicklaus who emerged on the golfing scene to dominate the game is among the innumerable great golfers who allow the left heel to be pulled up naturally on the backswing, something doubly advisable for someone of his build.

No two players necessarily sense the swing in quite the same way, but I agree with those who assert that an excellent tip for promoting the correct weight shift is that the weight goes on the backswing toward the toe of the left foot and the heel of the right and *vice versa* on the through swing.

The weight shift, it goes almost without saying, is bound up with footwork and Tommy Armour, without discounting its importance in other games such as tennis, cricket and baseball, averred that it mattered more in golf than any other sport. A sweeping statement, but it did underline how Armour, who for so long enjoyed the reputation of the greatest of all teachers, viewed the swing.

I myself am convinced that those who use their feet and legs correctly, and make the proper weight shift both going back and coming forward, have the choice of playing the game mainly with their hands as such as Henry Cotton have advocated, or using everything at their disposal, their legs and all the most powerful muscles in their body. The other side of that coin is that if the footwork and the leg action are inadequate, the weight shift faulty, the player has no alternative but to hit with his hands – and all too often his legs will have failed to put him in the best position to do so to the greatest effect.

WRIST POSITION

Great golfers have played great golf with the left wrist at the top of the backswing square, cupped or closed but what I call the hinged-door position at the top of the backswing is ruinous. One tell-tale facet of the hinged door is that the right wrist is straight while the symptoms can include a tendency to slap at the shot or to hit it off the nose. Sometimes, but not always, it originates in the takeaway and that is where I usually first look for the cause before widening the search.

With the left wrist clawed or closed, the player is virtually compelled to play from shut to open as Lee Trevino does. It is a strong man's action and, generally speaking, not for the older golfer and undeniably playing from shut to open adds to the chances of a player suffering from what is sometimes referred to as the golfer's occupational hazard, a bad back. Indeed, one of the great advantages of the contrasting method as advocated by Henry Cotton and others is that it does so much to render null and void that reference to "occupational hazard".

The left wrist square at the top is seen by many, including leading teachers and outstanding players, as the goal at which to aim and certainly there is nothing wrong with such a position. But, from my own experience, it is also best suited to those who have strength to spare and who, in their swing, are prepared to place much emphasis on the left arm and the back of the left hand in the downswing.

The ideal to me is a left wrist slightly cupped to the swing plane which is a position which blends perfectly with a good rotation of the left arm.

A little old-fashioned? Simply because it was favoured by so many of the legendary players of yesteryear does not make it wrong — something which, as more and more of today's golfers are coming to realise, applies to other areas of the swing where the eternal golfing verities have survived many a passing fad.

Sam Torrance just after the downswing has begun. Note the knees.

TEN

THE DOWNSWING

Those who see the backswing differently from me, who think of starting upstairs rather than downstairs, and of turning the torso and the shoulders against a resisting bottom half, still have a weight shift. Or, if they do not, take it from me they will not hit the ball to anywhere near their full potential.

Like Sam Snead, who was wont to practise in his bare feet if he lost the rhythm and feel of his swing, I believe that the swing begins from the ground up. Provided the left arm has rotated as it should, the golfer is a long way towards a backswing which will put him in great shape for the start of the downswing. But there has to be resistance from the right side if the power is to be stored.

Ideally, I like to see a golfer swing back against the resistance of a flexed right knee, but the great thing is to avoid the weight going over on to the outside of the right foot, which is why you will sometimes see golfers practising with the ancient device of having a golf-ball lodged under the right side of their right foot.

It has been said in various quarters that one thing which Ben Hogan got wrong in his classic treatise, *The Modern Fundamentals of Golf*, was that he attributed to stretched muscles an elasticity which they do not actually possess. Nevertheless, the coiled spring from which that notion of Ben Hogan's no doubt originated is a good image for the top of the swing. The suggestion of a recoil and release into impact, which the golfer could scarcely prevent even if he wanted to do so, is excellent.

Sam Torrance in a great position coming into impact. The right elbow is in to the side and the right knee bent as the right foot starts to give its additional push. Torrance's head is behind the ball and, though he is hitting against his left side, the left knee is still flexed. You can foresee both the explosion of power and the depth of the extension through impact.

Tom Watson with the legs very markedly leading into the downswing but the club-face a little more shut than is normally recommended for the majority of golfers.

Above left, Bob Torrance at the top of the backswing.

Above right, on the downswing.

Left, after impact.

THE DOWNSWING

Where many of the best golfers are concerned, once the backswing has been completed, the gun loaded, the requisite movement into impact long ago became instinctive. Yet, at all levels of the game from the lowliest to the most exalted, there are golfers who, not necessarily always but from time to time, need a thought with which to trigger the downswing.

Some, including Sam Snead, speak of pulling down with the left hand or at any rate the last two or three fingers; some, including the famed English amateur, Ronnie White, of returning the left heel to the ground, always assuming they have allowed it to be pulled up on the backswing; some, including both Bobby Jones and Ben Hogan, of leading the downswing with the hips; some, including the diminutive but long-hitting Bob Toski, of leading it with the left knee; and still others, including Tommy Armour, of making sure that the right knee gets into the shot. Any one of those can be used to cue the downswing successfully but the golfer will not necessarily stay with the same one all his days.

Of course, such movements are interrelated, and the golfer who pulls down with his left hand will thereby be simultaneously leading the downswing with his hips as the weight goes over to the left side. Similarly, the golfer who keys on getting his right knee into the shot will at the same time be clearing his left side.

Even the same action is subject to different interpretations. Lee Trevino talks of shooting with the hips. Stewart Maiden, the Scottish professional whose lovely swing Bobby Jones imitated as a small boy, contended that the turning of the hips toward the hole on the line of flight was the leading element in the downswing. The English-born professional, Harry "Lighthorse" Cooper, who made his name in America but whom Sam Snead, one night when he was holding court at Fulford, deemed the greatest striker he ever saw, maintained that the hips should lead the downswing but opined that their initial movement was diagonal before straightening towards the line of the hole and clearing to the left.

Ireland's Philip Walton, in whom Bob Torrance sees a Ryder Cup player of the future, badly needed to emphasise the role of the left arm more in his swing, to strengthen its contribution. Bob Torrance thought he had his fair share of swing flaws but that he had much going for him which can never be taught.

At the top

Downswing

Impact

Post-impact

The downswing, as most golfers have come to appreciate, begins before the backswing has been completed, and if executed powerfully and well can increase the degree of wrist cock through the additional tug it imposes. Ben Hogan's pronounced lateral drive with the hips is the best start to a downswing I ever saw. Masterly though I perceive it to be, I know, for instance, that it does not work for my son Sam, who does much better when thinking of driving into impact with his legs. The great thing about beginning the downswing downstairs – and never mind if that action in itself is initiated by the pulling down of the left hand, or, say, the returning of the right elbow into the side – is that it precludes the shoulders from taking over at the start of the downswing, other than which there is no more damaging fault.

Ben Hogan, with that exemplary hip drive of his, holds that the head is the captive of a good swing, and in the same camp is Neil Coles, who has asserted that if the legs lead the downswing the head has to stay back. The quintuple Open champion, the Australian Peter Thomson, and Tommy Armour see it the other way round, though the end product will not necessarily be so very different. Thomson has more than once touched on how he concentrates on the sensation of keeping his head behind the ball through impact, and I should say that if he does that then the bottom half is almost compelled to lead the forward momentum. A steady head was, in every sense, at the very hub of Tommy Armour's teaching, though it could be that the fact that he had lost an eye in the Kaiser's War made a still head an all the more desirable feature of his own swing.

The "soft" left knee through the hitting area favoured by many of the moderns is associated mostly with those who think of using the legs to drive into impact, but the fact that a player leads the downswing with his hips does not mean that he has perforce to hit against a straight left leg.

Bobby Jones called a correct start to the downswing the single most important movement. As he underlined, a golfer can do many things wrong and yet play acceptable golf if he just gets that one thing right.

Sam Torrance (left) being presented with an award by Tony Jacklin at the annual PGA European Tour dinner, one of the ceremonial occasions which marked the home-based Scottish tournament professional's 1984 season in which he won thrice on the European circuit.

Sam Torrance on the victory rostrum after winning the 1985 Johnnie Walker Monte Carlo Open with Isao Aoki second and Sandy Lyle third.

ELEVEN

HEEL TO TOE

"Heel and toe" as I use the term has nothing to do with footwork or the weight shift. Rather does it relate to the path on which the club-face comes into impact.

The opposite of a heel-to-toe golfer is, of course, a toe and heel player. Outstanding examples of the former would be Ben Hogan and Lee Trevino, of the latter such as Bobby Locke, Christy O'Connor senior and Jack Nicklaus.

A heel-to-toe player will normally leave a divot pointing approximately in the direction of three minutes to twelve, where that of the toe-to-heel player will point to three minutes past or still later on the clock if the player in question is the aforementioned Bobby Locke.

A heel-to-toe player, generally speaking, will be a body player, a toe-to-heel player more of an arms player, though Jack Nicklaus, who comes in the toe-to-heel category, is a bit of both. All other things being equal, the heel-to-toe player would flight the ball with a touch of fade, the toe-to-heel golfer with a hint of draw. Does it matter? To me it does because grasping the concept is all part of an understanding of the swing and, at least in the upper echelons of golf, among the professionals and the outstanding amateurs, knowing precisely what you are doing will enlighten rather than confuse. The player knows better what goes with what, what to guard against and what to strengthen.

A typical heel-to-toe player's finish.

The heel-to-toe player's divot running to three minutes to twelve.

A characteristic toe-to-heel
player's finish.

The toe-to-heel player's divot
running to three minutes past
twelve.

Sam Torrance past impact with the left arm just beginning to bend preparatory to folding in the follow-through and finish. Note the straight right arm and remember Ben Hogan's contention that, if the maximum width of arc were to be obtained, one or other arm must always be straight right through the swing, the left arm on the backswing and immediately through impact and the right arm in the follow-through.

TWELVE

IMPACT, FOLLOW-THROUGH AND FINISH

Plainly, the follow-through and finish can sometimes be a valuable indication of what happened in the swing and, as previously noted, a heel-to-toe player will tend to finish lower than a toe-to-heel. But there is a position beyond impact, at that moment when both arms are straight for the only time in the swing, which usually interests me much more and is apt to be more significantly revealing.

In that facet of the swing, you can see the difference which the big ball and the modern conditioning of courses have made to actions on this side of the Atlantic. In the old days, when our players were having to pick the small ball up off often parched, bare and hard seaside links, the right hand was wont to climb much more quickly over the left in the early stages of the follow-through. Altogether, a much more flicky action . . .

One of the currently fashionable teaching trends is the emphasis placed on the early folding of the left arm on the through swing, but it is not one of the planks on which I base my own teaching because, while it will help one player, it can restrict another. To put it another way, it is not something I would have all my pupils doing or thinking about, only some.

In considering impact and follow-through, I have not spoken of the supinating left wrist beloved of Ben Hogan, the wrist-bone high and the left wrist bowed out. It is a magnificent aid to great striking but, to me, the preserve of those who are not only technically very good but very strong.

101

Sam Torrance shows great extension and the long right arm advocated by Ben Hogan, the right hand now in the course of climbing over the left.

Of course, the last thing you want is to have the left wrist collapsing or pronating through impact, but the picture Hogan had and the position he achieved is, I am persuaded, beyond the reach of all but, in Churchill's phrase, "the few and and the very few".

Even for the professional golfer, let alone for the rank and file, it is better to think of the left hand taking the hit and, depending a little on the grip, on the back of the left hand being square to the line of flight. As always, it is a question of knowing what goes with what and what is, in that phrase of Deane Beman's, mutually exclusive.

Sam Torrance caught at the only moment in the swing when both arms are straight.

Just imagine if Lee Trevino, with that very "strong" grip of his but complementary late release, were to concentrate instead on having the left wrist supinating. The hooks which would result would be collectors' items. Yet Hogan much admires the fellow fader he sees in Trevino even though they go about achieving it so differently.

The instructional guideline that the position at address should as nearly as possible presage the position at impact is obviously open to an almost ludicrous exaggeration. Gary Player, for one, would look more than a little odd if he were to

Bernhard Langer, by far the greatest player to come out of Germany, hitting flat out. Observe the way the right knee and right foot have ensured that he got his right side into the shot, the left side having taken the hit with the sheer force rolling the left foot over on to its outside.

Sam Torrance. A glorious finish which speaks well of what had gone before.

set up to the ball in the outline of a Gary Player tearing flat-out through impact. Nonetheless, within reason, it is a sound and helpful conception.

The checkpoints in the matter of technique which I look for at impact are the result of what has gone before rather than specific positions which the player sets out to achieve on his or her own. If they are not all there, it behoves the teacher to work back to the flaw which is causing the absence of one or more.

At impact, I like to see the right elbow into the right side and still bent, for it is only after impact that the right arm straightens. The right leg must not straighten at impact, whatever you may have read in some of the old teaching treatises, but should be bent into the shot with, ideally, a definite push coming from the inside of the right foot.

Since I advocate that the ball position remains unchanged and inside the left heel for all standard shots, I can consequently have pupils who follow that stipulation having at impact a firm sensation of keeping the head behind the ball. Clearly, that becomes anatomically more difficult for those who move the ball back in their stance markedly as they go down through the clubs in the bag.

Such players focus on keeping the head still or at least quiet, though if the downswing begins downstairs as it should, the basic laws of balance will themselves do much to prevent the head from moving forward with the shot. The more natural the process the better, whether the player gives the impression of freewheeling through impact as did Bobby Jones, or exploding into impact in the inimitable manner of Arnold Palmer.

The heel-to-toe player, the body player, will have his hips open and the left hip cleared through impact, and even the shoulders a touch open, too. The hands player can achieve his effects with his shoulders still square to the line.

There are coaches who seek to have their pupils achieve a beautiful finish and work back from there on the grounds that, in order to get into that position, they must have done almost everything that went before correctly. Myself, I do not much care for it because, after all, look at the sometimes almost grotesque follow-throughs of Arnold Palmer and Gary Player, and those after some of their greatest shots.

The Scottish Squad: left to right: standing – George Ovens (SGU), Wayne Henderson (Montrose), Steven Rosie (Bathgate), Andrew Coltart (Thornhill), Stuart McGregor (Braehead), Michael Braidwood (Scotscraig), Drew Elliot (Fereneze), Simon Mackenzie (West Linton), Bob McLaren (SGU), Walter MacKay (SGU), Denis Miller (SGU President); crouching – Ross Aitken (Largs), Martin Hastie (St Andrews), Bob Torrance (National Coach), Stephen Docherty (Cruden Bay), Colin Fraser (Burntisland), Stuart Syme (St Andrews).

Peter Jacobsen, the American Ryder Cup player. This position can be equalled but not bettered. I like my pupils to imagine on the downswing that they have a sponge under the right armpit which will be squeezed as the right elbow comes into the side on the downswing. Jacobsen captures perfectly that action.

THIRTEEN

PUPILS

I kept an eye on Sam's golf from the day he started but not in the sense of keeping him in a coaching strait-jacket. To have done so might have ensured that he was always grammatically flawless but the free expression of his natural talent would very likely have been suffocated.

When he was a small boy, probably the most important thing I did for his golfing future was to cut down clubs for him so that, whatever else they were, they were always of the right length. Some great golfers may have had to make do at first with cast-down full-length clubs, but the great danger is that a child so equipped will develop perforce a very flat swing simply because that is the only way he can make room for himself to hit the ball.

Like many another youngster, Sam at one time had a very "strong" grip in terms of the amount of knuckle showing on the left hand and the degree to which the right hand was under. It is something from which even the offspring of professionals are not necessarily immune and, indeed, Arnold Palmer himself had to curb a marked inclination towards a hooker's hold on the club.

When Sam was moving from his teens into his twenties, he was troubled by a hook and many self-appointed pundits pointed knowingly to his grip. I was convinced that that tendency to hook could more often be traced to a faulty leg and foot action. Sam used to swing back with the left knee pointing almost straight forward rather than in behind the ball, and from there he would instinctively strive to clear himself on the downswing by spinning the hips fiercely and coming up on his toes at impact.

He was immensely long but, during a visit home to Largs in his spell as an assistant at Sunningdale, I explained to him that the time had come when we would have to do something about that flawed leg action. He tried what I suggested but, after a few shots, declared that he could not do it and that it was not for him. "Suit yourself," I said, and stomped back to the house.

The next morning Sam reappeared, apologising and confessing that he knew that it was a change which had to be made. Moreover, he accepted that initially he would lose quite a bit of length and would probably never get all of it back. Nor did he, but the point was that he could spare some yards and it was a price well worth paying for his much-improved accuracy.

Even in the days when his leg and foot action left so much to be desired, he somehow still succeeded in making a good weight shift and, since the remedial treatment, his weight transference has been one of the great strengths of his golf.

Of course, as with every other golfer, there have been little things which have gone wrong from time to time – little to the naked eye but frequently the difference between his hitting the ball at his best and striking it frustratingly indifferently. The most serious – and not just because, as old faults will, it was always apt to resurface – was the habit of allowing his hands to come apart at the top of the backswing. I have spoken elsewhere of outstanding golfers who permitted the club a certain amount of latitude in the right hand, but with Sam it coupled with a tendency to let the right elbow fly and so it was well worth taking the trouble to cure it. Not that we did anything very magical or original, the answer being the advice handed down over the generations to practise swinging with a coin pressed beneath the left thumb and the pad of the right hand.

Sam, in the days when his left knee shot virtually straight forward on the backswing, held his head stock still, but nowadays I would say that he has a quiet head rather than a stationary one. To the layman that may sound a mere matter of semantics, but there is a real difference between the often cramped swing of the player holding his head artificially still and the player allowing a certain tolerance.

There were periods in Sam's career when the weight transfer was so free as to be partially self-defeating in that there was no resistance from a flexed right knee and the weight was going over to the outside of the right foot. It goes almost without saying that that meant not only that it was not suitably stored but that it was very difficult for him to get it flowing back correctly into the downswing.

I had almost from the first done quite a bit of teaching of club golfers and I had enjoyed it, not least because I could fairly claim no small measure of success. Not that I knew in those days what I know now – not by many a mile – but rather that I seldom found it difficult to identify with another golfer's problems, to get on the same wavelength.

However, in the Northern Open of 1981, I was drawn with the Lancastrian, Derrick Cooper. Though he won that year at Royal Dornoch, he was far from happy with his swing, after a sojourn in America in connection with an ambitiously flamboyant bid by a Welsh businessman to produce a world-class champion out of a picked squad of promising young players. In the Glasgow Open at Haggs Castle that summer, Derrick missed the cut and was in such despair over his game that it could only have been a matter of time before he turned his back on a career as a tournament professional. He asked if I would have a look at him and, after just one lesson, he returned south to win a pro-am with a 13-under-par round of 57 – an astonishing feat which brought from my wife, June, the apprehensive remark that she just hoped that he wouldn't expect to keep up the same rate of improvement with every lesson.

A good enough footballer to have had trials with Rochdale, Preston North End and Bolton Wanderers before golf claimed

Bill Longmuir (left) with Bob Torrance and John O'Leary. The dragging of the clubhead in the takeaway, which had been a feature of the swings of such all-time greats in the days of the hickory shaft as Harry Vardon and Bobby Jones, did not work for Longmuir, while O'Leary, a talented all-round sportsman, had got into the habit of aiming ten yards right of target even with an eight-iron.

him for its own, Cooper was strongly built and not short of ball-sense, but I have seldom seen a golfer, in the old phrase, so fouled up in the mechanics of the game. He had become horribly wooden as he sought awkwardly to make the movements he had had instilled into him in America. There were so many things wrong that the trick was knowing where to start.

I began by helping him with his set-up wherein his back had become very bent and his head too stooped and low, but the main thing I did was to work on his weight transfer with that left knee coming in behind the ball and the right hip clearing. The effect was almost instantaneous, Derrick exclaiming that he felt "the freedom of a man suddenly released from jail".

Other adjustments followed: a widening of the stance, the grip of the right hand moved more into the fingers from the palm, and a rotation of the left arm on the backswing which did much to ensure that the left wrist was square at the top. Another outcome of that rotation of the left arm was that if Derrick still crossed the line he did so less markedly and in a position in relation to his shoulders a lot more reminiscent of, for example, Bobby Jones than the high-above-the-head slant in which I had found him at Haggs Castle.

On the subject of crossing the line, too many great players have done it for it to be wrong in itself, and the fact that Derrick was given to doing so was, to my mind, the least of his worries. At any rate, no man ever had a more grateful pupil and he never ceases to stress, knowing the appeal of length to golfers, that the changes I wrought in his swing released 30 or 40 yards which had been stifled in his old swing.

The pronounced improvement in Derrick's golf, taken in conjunction with the fact that Sam's swing was widely admired, soon led to requests from other professionals for me to work with them. Bill Longmuir and John O'Leary were particular friends of Sam's and so it was natural enough that they should be among the first.

When he came to me, Bill had just missed nine cuts in a row. He was technically in deep trouble though, obviously, he had the ability to play really good golf even if the temperament to see a tournament right down to the wire has never come easily to him. Yet his besetting sin, in that it did not work for him, was something which the old-timers, particularly going back to the days of hickory shafts, would have seen as a virtue. Namely, his dragging of the clubhead in the takeaway.

From that start, he had the club-face very open at the top with the left wrist hinging like a door. To me it is the right wrist which should hinge like a door, and though the left wrist can do so too, it must break to the swing plane. To hit the ball well from that top-of-the-swing position, Bill had to get his hands into the act to an inordinate extent with a very definite crossing of the right hand over the left in the follow-through. Any mistiming and almost anything could happen from a snap hook to hitting it right off the snout.

The basic alteration he had to make was to get the clubhead away earlier in the backswing, the effect being close to the conventional one-piece takeaway. For a time, his staple shape of shot was a fade and, as you would expect, he felt very safe with that flight but eventually decided it was costing him too many yards. Posture and the weight shift were also areas of his action which needed attention but, fundamentally, it was those first six inches away from the ball which were make or break for him.

John O'Leary had been to some distinguished teachers before he came under my wing. Even so, he had got into the habit of aiming well to the right and swinging the club very much round his backside with, considering that he was such a gifted all-round sportsman, a disappointing absence of footwork. He was aiming, I swear, ten yards right with an eight-iron and I said to him, bluntly, "If you are doing that now, how far off line do you think you'll be aiming in two years?"

His mental picture of the swing, as viewed from vertically above, was of something not far removed from a circle, but he responded to my suggestion that that was much too extreme and that it would pay him to straighten out the circle till it was oblong.

With the swing he had, the only way he could clear himself

Bob Torrance steadies the head of Ireland's David Feherty. Torrance believes in a "quiet" head but maintains that it is a mistake to attempt to hold it rigidly stock still. A model pupil with much innate ability, Feherty was made to practise swinging with a small towel tucked under each armpit, a device which compels a greater synchronisation of a golfer's top half and bottom.

for the hit was by coming up on his toes at impact. Bobby Jones did that when hitting flat out and many of the great players on the distaff side of golf have done it too, one explanation often advanced being that they mostly have to contend with much more in the way of a bust than is the lot of men. I do not

Bob Torrance adjusts the angle of the club in the set-up of Wayne Westner, a South African who returned home to win his country's Open Championship after tuition from the Largs professional. Weight transference was his problem and Bob Torrance had him swinging back, by way of a practice device, with his left foot actually coming off the ground.

Sandy Lyle. A deceptive picture in that the use he makes of his legs is much less obviously pronounced than in many another golfer and yet, make no mistake, they are a primary source of his often awesome length, particularly with his Ping one-iron. Because of his particular leg action, he has more of a tendency than most other leading professionals to let the shoulders into the act too early on the downswing, which can lead to the angle of attack into impact being insufficiently inside the backswing's width of club-head arc. Bob Torrance suggested a slight lateral movement at the start of the downswing as the appropriate antidote for this enviably gifted and distinguished pupil.

condemn it wholesale, and if I had an amateur who was hitting the ball well despite such an action, I should almost certainly leave him or her alone. But personally I think that, despite the triumphant record of Bobby Jones which any professional would love to have owned, a golfer who fights par for a living had better be more solidly planted through the hitting area.

John improved dramatically in our early months together and little more than 12 weeks after we first joined forces, he won the Irish Open. He has a lot of talent but, like so many others, he is a different player when in good physical condition and with a clear mind free to concentrate on the round in hand.

John's compatriot, David Feherty, who won the 1986 Scottish Open, has a great deal of God-given ability but Irishmen, for better or worse, are more liable to grow up playing by the light of nature than the sons and daughters of other golfing lands. David had lost it somewhere along the line, his top half and his bottom half being strangely disconnected in terms of the swing, the whole action decidedly flat-footed. The antidote for him took the form of a small towel tucked under each arm, a device which compels a far greater synchronisation of upstairs and downstairs.

With David I went so far as to encourage him to make what felt like a lateral movement amounting to a sway. Not that he was really swaying, simply that it felt like that to him after so many years without a proper weight transference.

In his grip, the club ran across the breadth of the palm of his left hand and so the angle had to be altered in order that it ran across the palm more diagonally. The right hand was too far under and had to be turned a little anti-clockwise. Still with the grip, I gave him a shorter left thumb, a change no less a personage than Ben Hogan also made in radically altering his swing when his career had already attained heights which would have more than satisfied other men.

Feherty is an excellent pupil and he is aware that the next step is to widen his swing a little more, make it a shade more upright and encourage a hand action at the top in which the wrists cock still further in the start of the downswing. The Americans talk more and more of transition and it is a good word to capture that moment when the backswing and downswing melt the one into the other.

Many speak of tempo and mean by their use of the word a slow and leisurely swing. Yet that is nonsense because, by that token, Ben Hogan with his relatively swift swing had none and Sam Snead had it all. To me, tempo is the perfect flow of the backswing into the downswing. If that happens, no matter the pace of the swing, a golfer can be sure there is nothing wrong with his tempo.

Yet another Irishman among my clientèle is Philip Walton, a Walker Cup player in both 1981 and 1983 and a young man who was three years on a college golf scholarship in Oklahoma. He was one more professional who favoured a takeaway which was too much on the inside, but that was not what made him a particularly interesting case. Rather was it that his left arm needed strengthening in the sense of being emphasised more in the pattern of his swing. It was not a matter of physically strengthening the left arm, but rather of making sure that it played a more positive role, with Philip "thinking" left arm and back of the left hand in his attack on the ball. It was medicine he badly needed, for when we first got together he was even prone to shanking.

He was noticeably shut at the top of the backswing. By showing him how to rotate his left arm on the backswing, it was not difficult to get him into a much better position at the top, but there was still the question of a grip which was threateningly "strong". Once more, taking just one step at a time, I had him hitting balls for a couple of days, concentrating on that rotation of the left arm. They flew powerfully but too many of them were hooked as, of course, was to be expected. Now was the time to ask for that comparatively slight but important "weakening" of the grip and at once he was nailing ball after ball with just the flight he wanted.

Wayne Westner was a South African who had coughed up

A superb action photograph of the pocket Hercules that is the five foot, four and a half inch Ian Woosnam halfway through the downswing which has very obviously begun downstairs in the feet, legs and hips. The right elbow is already tucking itself into the side and the power is still stored in the fully retained wrist cock. It is power personified and, though Woosnam always points to the strength emanating from a boyhood spent working on the farm as the explanation of his length, everyone knows muscular, much larger, manual workers who can yet hardly hit the ball out of their shadow. To no small extent, natural clubhead speed is something with which you are born, and Bob Torrance can think of no more notable example of one with what he calls the essential "swipe" in his swing than the diminutive Welshman.

Ian Woosnam at the top of the swing, the one minor criticism being that the weight has shifted a little to the outside of the right foot. Woosnam, under Torrance, has worked with much success on keeping the right knee flexed on the backswing to obtain the necessary resistance. Many small men have indulged in personal idiosyncrasies in order to obtain what they felt was the necessary width of arc. That great little battler, the Walker Cup Scot, Sandy Saddler, sometimes put onlookers in mind of a batsman in the world of cricket moving on to the back foot. Woosnam, though, achieves his effects and remarkable distance without resort to the unorthodox or unconventional.

30,000 dollars for tuition in Florida but his hip action was all wrong, a form of reverse pivot which made him what I would call a stubby hitter of a golf-ball. He made no room on his backswing for the downswing and clearly he had to discover what a transference of weight from left to right and right to left felt like. Different exercises work for different people, and what I had Wayne doing was swinging back with his left foot coming off the ground prior to his downswing into impact. On that line of teaching, I would add that another instructive exercise, though this time with regard to the weight shift on the through swing, is to hit five-irons and, by way of the follow-through, take a step forward with the right foot. Wayne, incidentally, was quickly rewarded with the South African Open title.

During the Bell's Scottish Open on the King's Course of the Gleneagles Hotel, Gordon Brand, the professional at Knowle and a noted teacher in his own right, asked me for a second opinion on his son's swing. Gordon Brand junior had not been completely comfortable in his shot-making and there is always a chance that a fresh eye will more readily detect cause and effect.

It seemed to me that Gordon, a class player with basically a very fine swing, was a little too shut at the top. Although I did not doubt that with his gift for the game he would still play some wonderful stuff when hot, I thought it inevitable that from that top-of-the-swing position he would be erratic.

Yet again nothing more than the correct rotation of the left arm on the backswing was enough to put right that worryingly shut club-face at the top, but at first he was looking to get the club into the slot at the top merely with his arms. The next stage was to make sure that the body turned in harmony with that rotation of the left arm, and one helpful tip in achieving that can be to make a deliberate attempt to keep the space between the arms and the ribs constant in the backswing turn. You probably will not achieve it but it is a very worthwhile exercise.

Stage three for Gordon was a matter of improving his hip turn, his right hip moving laterally and finishing high on the backswing rather than maintaining the same level and clearing. All told, there was quite a lot for him to think about, but he is not just an outstanding player but a very good pupil and if he sticks to the task, it should all soon become second nature to him.

Sandy Lyle is another son of a professional who was taught by his father, Alex Lyle, the professional at Hawkstone Park and a member of the famous Clober golfing dynasty. I do not doubt that if Alex were within reach Sandy would always turn to him first but, when he is on tour, he has always known that he has his father's blessing to pull in for a swing service with the likes of myself, America's Jim Ballard or Dave Leadbetter. At the Dunhill Cup one year, Sandy, one of the most awesome sights in golf when he has a one-iron in hand, came to me for help, aware that something was wrong but unable to decide quite what it was.

If you were to trace the outline of a good player's backswing from, in cricketing parlance, point – in other words, from bang opposite the golfer – and then trace the path of his downswing, the latter would be well inside the former. What Sandy was doing was turning his shoulders as the first movement of the downswing rather than the second – that is after the swing had begun downstairs – and so his downswing gave the impression of actually being outside his backswing in terms of those aforesaid traced paths.

With most players, I should have looked to cure it by ensuring the start of the backswing was made with the hips or the legs but, where Sandy was concerned, I found it easier to remedy the much too shallow attack he was making on the ball by getting him to make a lateral movement before the shoulders began to turn back. The right elbow now came into the side where the right arm had been tending to straighten prematurely and the angle of attack was once again neither too steep nor too horizontal.

Ian Woosnam had a phenomenal year in 1987 when he won over a million pounds around the world but, in the early months, he had his problems. He stands only five feet four and a half inches and was giving away what height he had by errors in his posture. He needed to stand up, lean forward from the waist and then flex his knees. If he did it the other way round and began by sitting into his knee flex, he never got it right.

Once he had sorted out his posture, there was the matter of the weight shift which, in turn, led to my working on the action of his hips. A failure to clear his right hip gave him a movement into impact in which his stomach thrust forward toward the ball, though it was a more subtle and less easily detected flaw than those bare words suggest. Once he had his left knee and right hip doing as they should on the backswing, his extraordinary power had free rein and the golf he played throughout 1987 was something to behold.

In August the following year, he was at Turnberry for the BBC Pro-Celebrity series and I noticed that, from straight in front, the outside of his left thumb was visible in his grip. I got him to place it less on top of the shaft and more to the right side. The rest of his left hand had not really changed position but he said at once that his left hand grip now felt alarmingly strong. When he hit shots with it, he admitted at once that it felt good but he was still uneasy about the change until I showed him what it looked like on video. He was no less amazed at how good it looked than he had been at how good it felt.

It has been said that a man can play fine golf all his life with nothing but backswing thoughts in that if the backswing is right the rest is little more than an automatic release. That is going a little too far because many a golfer needs a thought with which to trigger the downswing, Woosnam himself being on record as saying that he pulls down with the left hand. Not that the same player will always have the same thought even for the same action.

The point is that once the downswing has begun there is little, if anything, the player can do to save it if it is wrong. That is not to say, mind you, that a player like Billy Casper has not benefited from having in his mind's eye a picture of his right

Jill Kinloch, a promising tennis player, in which realm she was the Scottish Under-14 Grass Courts champion, sought out Bob Torrance on switching to golf. Winning a golf scholarship to an American university, she has played most of her recent golf on the other side of the Atlantic but continues to repair to the Largs guru on every visit home. What Torrance liked about her from the start was that, whatever her technical deficiencies when she first came to him, she always had in her swing a God-given hit.

hand climbing over his left in the follow-through where, in his younger days, that same image was of the left hand almost blocking the ball through impact.

I have long maintained that if a player has to hold anything back, a muscle, bone or what have you, as he explodes through impact, then there is something wrong with his swing and professional and pupil must work back to discover what. It was revealing, during a Benson & Hedges at Fulford, to find that, once I had got the former Australian Open champion, Peter Fowler, to make the proper weight transference on the backswing, he almost at once had the feeling that he was getting everything into the shot, including a previously somewhat dormant right side.

Russell Weir, a PGA Cup player who has dominated Scotland's tartan tour in recent seasons, is a former Scottish Boys' champion who was virtually out of the game for some years and who, when he came to me, described his game as being in an awful mess. He is a real golfer, though, and we worked for seven hours on that first Saturday and for eight hours on the Sunday.

There was a lot to be done. His hands had to fit more snugly together on the grip, his stance was a little too narrow, his takeaway had to be rather straighter back. He needed to pivot better with regard to the transference of weight and to use his hips to initiate the downswing. He was such a receptive pupil that I should be surprised if he is not now, besides being a very useful tournament player, a very sound teacher.

Still among my brother Scots, Ian Young was a player who responded well to the old Ben Hogan exercise of swinging, by way of a practice ploy, with the elbows clamped to the sides, an exercise which forces the torso and the leg action to work together.

Ladies are obviously anatomically a bit different but the eternal golfing verities still hold for them. One of my most intriguing pupils was Jill Kinloch, who had been a promising tennis player before her parents decided that temperamentally she was probably better suited to golf. She required a lot done to her swing but the great thing about her from the first was that, even though she cut across every shot, she had what I call the swipe but which is more grandly termed the basic clubhead speed. She stayed in touch even when she went to college in America and her winning of Scotland's Highland Open was another step in the right direction.

Celebrities can be a cross between your rank-and-file club golfer and your professional in that they have many of the problems of the first category but a great deal in common also with the second. They usually play much of their golf in the public eye and are usually the recipients of all manner of assorted well-meaning advice.

Yet even such a proficient golfer as Cliff Thorburn was recently standing so badly to the ball, tucking his posterior in rather than, as Sam Snead once graphically instructed President Eisenhower to do, sticking it out, that you could have tip-toed up behind him and pushed him over with the proverbial feather. The recipe for him was to keep the back straight, the head up, his backside out and his knees slightly flexed. When he did that he no longer was inclined to have too much weight on his heels but where I argue that it should be – on the heels and balls of the feet but not so much on the heels as to deprive the player of the feeling that he could, if he were barefoot, curl his toes to grip the turf.

Sean Connery was perhaps the prime example in my teaching of a player whose game stood to be transformed by a change of posture. He had been a disciple of Ben Hogan but what had worked for perhaps the greatest striker the game has seen had not worked for him. In particular, this tall and well-built man required to stand up to the ball but then to lean forward from the waist, thereby promoting a rather steeper shoulder plane and more upright swing. Once he had attended to those preliminary details, he soon got the idea of the leg and hip action necessary on the backswing to make room and time for the downswing.

Bob Torrance (left) with Russell Weir, nowadays a leading personality on Scotland's domestic circuit, the tartan tour. A former Scottish Boys' champion, Weir came to Torrance with problems in his swing after being virtually out of golf for some seasons and that weekend teacher and pupil worked together seven hours on the Saturday, eight on the Sunday.

Bob Torrance (left) with Roger Chapman. The former English Walker Cup player has become, as a professional, a prime example of the value of acquiring left arm rotation on the backswing, a new-found confidence oozing from the feeling he now has that he is "in the slot" at the top.

England's Barry Lane (left) with Bob Torrance at the 1988 Bell's Scottish Open over the King's Course of the Gleneagles Hotel. Lane won in great style and afterwards publicly thanked Bob Torrance, who had cured a disturbing tendency to hook or block by showing him how to marry his hand action in the hitting area to the turning back of the body in the downswing.

The effect was quite remarkable. He had always had a grip which was one hundred per cent right and now that grip was feeding off the requisite chain reaction, he could at last, in golfing terms, punch his weight.

Sean has played opposite some sensational damsels in his time but none, I wager, succeeded in producing quite the gleam he had in his eye the afternoon at Largs when he was hitting the ball so well that I decided to measure his shots. His six-iron came out at 200 yards, his drive at 280.

Derrick Cooper, the 33-year-old professional at Warrington's Birchwood Club, is congratulated by Bob Torrance on his maiden victory on the European Tour, the 1988 Cepsa Madrid Open. Aside from Bob's son, Sam, Cooper was the first professional to travel to Largs for regular lessons from Bob Torrance and, after the first such session, returned south to record a 13-under-par 57 in his next competitive round.

Anders Forsbrand whom Bob Torrance believes to be the best of the Swedes, a player of outstanding potential. When he first came to Bob Torrance, he was struggling against the insidious effects of a bad posture at address in which, viewed from the back of the tee, he looked, in Bob Torrance's words, "like a huge C".

Downhill

Align yourself to the slope but do not concentrate on being perpendicular to it at the cost of balance. Play the ball back in an open stance and make sure that you stay down on the shot with the club going through the ball. The shot will tend to slice, so aim left.

THE TRUTH ABOUT LIES

Uphill

Set yourself to the slope with the emphasis again on balance and the ball forward in the stance. Hit with the slope and, because the shot will tend to hook, adjust your aim accordingly. Just as in the choice of club off a downhill lie, the fact that the ball will come out lower has to be set against the fact that it will slice so, in an uphill lie, the shot's higher flight will have to be weighed against the element of hook. Obvious factors to be taken into consideration are the severity of the slope, wind and whether the turf on which it will alight is soft or firm.

Sidehill: Ball below feet

As in all the shots off slopes, this is a stroke in which to reduce the body movement and leg action, making it more a hands and arms shot. Balance is again a vital key, with the weight a little back on the heels. If the ball is well below the feet, do not overdo the flex of the knees but instead bend more from the waist. The shot, if correctly played, will fade and so, once more, the aim has to be suitably altered.

Sidehill: Ball above feet

Where, with the ball below the feet, you will want to grip at the very end of the club, with the ball above the feet you should choke down on the grip. Staying in balance with the weight very much on the balls of the feet, and playing the shot mainly with the hands and arms, you can expect the shot to draw which, of course, affects your alignment and aim.

Grass lying against you
The grass is going to get between club-face and ball whether you like it or not. Play it very much as you would a bunker shot and bear in mind that you will get comparatively little run.

Grass lying with you
This time make sure that you take the ball first while consciously guarding against the very real danger of the club bouncing and the shot being skinned. Take into account the obvious possibility of getting a flier.

Ball in divot hole

Since the important thing is to make sure you take the ball first, before the club catches the ground, play the ball back in the stance with the club squared. The swing will be steep with the hands leading through impact.

Ball perched in the rough

The risks here are that the ball will inadvertently be moved at the address and the club will pass under the ball at impact. Address the ball with the club hovering at the appropriate height and, even though it may be an iron that you are playing, sweep it away almost as you would a driver.

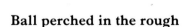

The Tilt
A faulty weight transference and flawed hip action have had their effect on the shoulder turn. No power has been stored for the downswing which cannot help but be uncertain and erratic.

CAUSE AND EFFECT

The Dip
The player has failed to maintain his height on the backswing with the left shoulder dipping towards the ball which has caused far too much weight to be upon the left foot. The so-called reverse pivot is the sure consequence, with the player falling back at impact.

Rolling

The left heel has screwed outwards causing the upper body to roll. It can still be a powerful action and there was an element of it in the swing of that celebrated Ulsterman, Fred Daly, the 1947 Open champion, but for most golfers it breeds inconsistency with the player brilliant one moment, all over the place the next.

Hit fat

Hitting fat, catching the ground before the ball, is another of golf's more grievous shots which can have assorted causes. For instance, a swing that fails to stay adequately centred through too much movement of the head; a dipping of the left shoulder on the backswing or an exaggerated dropping of the right shoulder on the through swing; or bad weight transference. However, I contend that most of such shots come from the right hand: hitting too early with it, over using it or allowing the arm to straighten prematurely.

Topping

This is usually attributed, particularly by your playing companions, to lifting your head but that in itself will have been caused either by coming up on the shot rather than staying down on it or by having stooped so low at address that you are almost bound to straighten up in the course of the swing. It can stem, too, from coming over the top in the downswing. The best cure is to check your posture at address and to make sure that your bottom half, your feet and legs, are working.

Skying

Sometimes known as a Gladys, the skied drive is nine times out of ten the result of falling into the shot to produce a steep chop. The remedy is yet again to make sure that the downswing begins downstairs, though the cure can begin still earlier by avoiding an abrupt pick-up on the backswing. A good, wide backswing and a quiet head will in themselves make this humiliating shot that much more unlikely.

The Draw

Stand closed with the shoulders correspondingly aligned and the ball, relatively, brought back a little in the stance. The face of the club is square to the line of play. The adjustments will promote the necessary in-to-out swing path which, in turn, produces the desired right-to-left spin. Some players will also "strengthen" the grip by turning their hands on the club a fraction clockwise but trial and error on the practice ground will soon tell you whether that is for you.

SHAPING THE SHOT

The Fade

Open up the stance with the shoulders once more following the alignment of the feet. The face of the club is square to the line of play. Such a set-up will give you the necessary out-to-in swing path which engenders the left to right flight you seek. Again, there are players who will also "weaken" the grip by turning their hands on the club a touch anti-clockwise and once more you can find out on the practice ground if that is the answer for you. Certainly, there are many golfers at all levels who prefer to leave the grip undisturbed.

Holding it down.

Hitting it high.

There is a wise old saying which some latter-day teachers have espoused as their own but which the late Sir Henry Cotton maintained dated back to the days of Harry Vardon: namely, when hitting into the wind, seek to hit the ball not harder but better. It is excellent advice, and an obvious corollary of the priciple that you are much better taking a couple of clubs more and hitting the ball easily, while simultaneously keeping it down, than hitting it hard and having it thereby climbing with fierce backspin. The player wishing to hold the ball down into the wind will want to move the ball back in his stance with the clubface appropriately squared and with the hands ahead of the ball at address and through impact.

Downwind, when you are looking to get the ball up, a more lofted club may often be all you need – a three-wood, say, rather than a driver. Nevertheless, there are occasions when you wish to hit the ball high, be it windy or not, when technique will come into it. You should move the ball forward in the stance with the weight rather more on the right side. The rest of the set-up virtually takes care of itself if you simply "think high".

Cross-winds are the greatest test of a player's ability to flight the ball. The club golfer usually does best when he simply aims off and allows for the wind, though a cross-wind can still play havoc with his game if he has either an habitual hook or a slice. For a good player, the decision is always whether to hold the ball up in the wind or borrow it, his ability to fade or draw the ball at will affording him the choice. Much will depend on whether he needs the length available by harnessing his shape of shot to the slant of the wind and also, of course, on the particular nature of the terrain and the trouble.

FOURTEEN

PITCHING AND CHIPPING

In the days of niblick rather than wedge, the player looked to obtain checking spin by standing open and cutting across the ball at impact. Today, all too many still imagine that to be the standard pitch and thereby make the shot unnecessarily and hazardously complicated.

Believing as I do that the more you can play every shot with basically the same swing, the more consistent you are likely to be, I have always seen the pitch, at any rate with the modern pitching-wedges and sand-wedges, as merely a modified version of the full shot.

Personally, I have never been convinced of the need to open the stance. Yet I do not quarrel with those who open up their whole set-up slightly or with those who keep their shoulders square while, in order still to help get the left hip out of the way and make it easier for the club to go through towards the flag, opening up their actual stance. If that suits them, fine – and, certainly, they have on their side the sheer weight of numbers.

In the shorter shots around the green, the better player not only has his hands a bit ahead of the ball but sits into the shot with his weight instinctively favouring his left side. For the handicap golfer, such a disposition of the weight has to be a matter of conscious thought until it becomes instinctive because, unlike the good player who trusts the club, the lesser golfer has usually to fight an impulse to help get the ball into the air by scooping it.

An exemplary illustration of Sam Torrance playing a wedge. His head is still looking at the spot where the ball was, the legs have clearly played their part in the stroke and the left side – with particular reference to the left arm and hand – has taken the hit. No scooping here.

If the player has set up too open, he will have almost no alternative but to hit the ball with left-to-right spin, but the basic stroke nowadays, and the stronger shot, is to flight the pitch with a shape which is either neutral or even touched with draw. However fast they are to putt, the conditioning and watering of today's greens mean that you seldom encounter the glorified table-tops of yesteryear and good contact with the modern wedge, even without square grooves, will ensure plenty of "stop".

Many years ago the late Dai Rees opined that we would never match the Americans until we learned how to use the legs in our short approaches, pitches and chips. How right he has proved to be, for you see it in the actions of all the best short-game exponents on the European tour, the advent of the big ball having helped.

In the modern pitch or short approach, there is weight transference and, unless the knees are appropriately flexed at the address, that rhythmic transfer of weight is likely to prove uncommonly difficult to achieve. Next time you are spectating, note how much more readily the player who gets his right knee into the shots around the green has the clubhead continuing on towards the target in goodly measure.

Of course, there are still times when the player will want to stand open, lay the club-face open and cut the legs from under the ball much in the mode of the old-timers. Again, a seasoned master such as Neil Coles can get very close to that image of a butterfly with sore feet alighting gingerly with the soft lob he plays by passing through impact at an unhurried and even pace.

There are times, too, such as when punching the ball under the branches of a tree or holding it down in the wind, when the player will want to move the ball back in his stance with the club-face squared but with the hands well ahead of the ball at address and through impact.

The pitch-and-run can sometimes be more easily played with, for instance, an eight- or nine-iron than a wedge, though much, obviously, will depend on the terrain and its contours and how much green the player has with which to play.

Sam Torrance chipping

The great pitchers have mostly been those who picked their spot and, picturing the flight and roll to a nicety, landed the ball either on it or suitably close. Much the same applies to the chip, whether the player is virtually a one-club chipper or one who prefers to stick very much to the same fundamental chipping action with the choice of club governing trajectory and roll.

As in the pitch, the majority of players like to open up a little, though once again I do not think it is essential. Once again, too, the weight will be favouring the left foot and the hands a little ahead of the ball.

The traditional chip, played with a club of no great loft, is much less frequently seen these days, partly because of the more receptive condition of the greens. To me, it is no coincidence that Bobby Locke, a deadly chipper but one who almost always favoured the wedge, was a great advocate of watered greens, albeit they did also clearly make it easier for him to hold them from afar with his draw.

For the club golfer who is having trouble with his chipping, I still often recommend his taking his five-iron and playing the shot virtually as a long putt, possibly even to the extent of changing from his normal grip to the reverse overlap he uses on the green. The professionals and the best amateurs, though, have almost blended their chipping into their pitching, save that most of them still employ far less wrist action in the chip than they do in the pitch.

Pitching and chipping are apt to be a very individual business. A player like Tom Watson likes mostly to play the little shots around the green without spin as an aid to getting consistency in terms of the degree of roll. In contrast, Bobby Locke gave the impression of often playing his with a touch of hooking spin, while Neil Coles plays his with seemingly just a hint of cut so that they always seem to check and roll to the same relentlessly repetitive pattern.

The real wizards in the departments of pitching and chipping take everything into account in terms of the lie and the terrain, the wind and the weather, but so do many others who, though

Above left, Sam Torrance at the top of the
backswing for a chip.

Above right, Sam Torrance at the top of
his backswing in playing a full pitch.

Right, Sam Torrance after impact on a
chip. The left hand has led the shot and is
still in control with the clubhead low to the
ground.

Sam Torrance, beginning the downswing for a pitch.

technically apparently their equals, are nowhere near as good.

The difference? Simply a question of golfing imagination, the ability to picture the shot – to "see" it.

Bruce McAllister (left) with Bob Torrance. Bruce is now an assistant at Turnberry after six years with Bob Torrance at Routenburn. "Nobody," reckons Bob Torrance, "could ask for a better or more willing assistant."

Sam Torrance holing from sand for an eagle at the second hole at Augusta in the 1983 US Masters.

FIFTEEN

BUNKER PLAY

Rembrandt might have told you how he painted, but that assuredly does not mean he could have taught you to paint like him. Much the same, in terms of bunker play, would apply to that wizard of the sand, Gary Player – and, for that matter, to such bunker exponents as Seve Ballesteros, Sandy Lyle and my own lad, Sam.

No less than the short-game magicians, great bunker players are born with much of what it takes already in them, and I should wager that none of the above ever had the slightest fear of sand from the day he first stepped into a bunker. However, do not despair, for the right technique and diligent practice can make you an adequate bunker player and maybe even tap rather more in the way of natural feel and talent than you would have supposed.

For the conventional greenside bunker recovery, set up open and swing down the line of your set-up but with the face of your sand-wedge so open that the ball will come out towards your target rather than in the direction of your swing path.

The ball should be forward in your stance but still inside the left heel, the weight rather more on the left foot and, for all that it is mostly a hands-and-arms shot, the knees flexed so that there will still be some natural flow downstairs.

If I have a hobby horse, it is that all too many golfers overdo both the extent to which they open up the stance and the steepness of the descent into impact.

149

Above left, Sam Torrance: address for standard bunker shot.

Above right, start back.

Left, half-way back.

Above left, at the top.

Above right, starting down.

Right, coming into impact.

Follow-through   *Finish*

As almost all golfers know, Gene Sarazen is the man generally credited with the invention of the sand-wedge with "bounce" on the sole, the trailing edge lower than the leading. He loved to relate how he got the idea from a flight in a small plane and the action of the ailerons.

The bounce or flange does much to stop the club from digging into the sand, and that is one reason why I hold that the angle of attack should be consistent with the need to skip or skim the ball out on a comparatively shallow divot of sand. Of course, there are particular shots when that shallow divot would not be applicable, such as when the ball has to be popped up quickly out of a deepish bunker and the player opts for a more abrupt visit to the sand with the bottom of the arc less rounded, more pointed.

The player has to wriggle his feet into the sand, which will give him the necessary firm footing and a further gauge of the sand's consistency. Since he has thus sunk a little, he should go down the shaft, while bearing in mind that he will want the club to pass under the ball.

The set-up will take care of the swing's plane and path for the orthodox bunker stroke, the player being free to give much of his concentration to just where the club is going to strike the sand and to the need to go through the shot with the left hand playing its part in keeping the club-face open. If the club-face closes, it will dig down, bounce or no bounce.

There is more than one opinion on how to control distance from a bunker: by increasing or decreasing the distance behind the ball the sand is struck, by always taking the same amount of sand and simply hitting harder, by the extent to which the set-up and the club-face are opened, or by the length of the swing. My own belief is that the best bunker players come to use a combination of all those elements wedded to years of experience and their own inherent eye and touch.

Not all sand is the same, and my own rule of thumb for the powdery variety, for example, is to aim to take less sand with the recovery than I normally would in order to finish up taking very much the usual amount. In wet sand, it is sometimes possible to play the ball almost as you would a fairway pitch or chip, contacting it first. But even where that is not possible, it often pays to put away the sand-wedge and play the shot with the sharper nip of a nine-iron.

Particularly when new sand has just been added to a bunker, the player will often encounter plugged lies, and the procedure then is to play the ball back in the stance with the club-face square. The shot itself has to be played with a steep pick-up, a brusque chop with almost no follow-through, the player having to keep in his mind's eye the fact that the ball will come out low and running.

Sam Torrance, address for standard bunker shot.

Start back.

Half-way back.

Top of the backswing.

Above left, start of the downswing.

Above right, coming into impact.

Right, follow-through.

Plugged lie

If the ball is in a so-called poached-egg lie, the important thing is to make sure that the clubhead passes beneath the whole of the little crater rather than coming through the sand into daylight before probably catching the ball somewhere around its equator.

If the lie is downhill, the golfer has to align himself to the slope with the weight more on the left foot and the ball back in his stance. My own preference is to set the club-face square for such a shot, but you should know that many notable bunker players would still choose to keep it a little open.

The danger is that the club will bounce on the sand and the ball be bladed either into the bunker face or clean across the green. Consequently, make sure that you take enough sand and that, just as with a shot elsewhere on the course off a downhill lie, the path of the club through impact follows the slope.

On an upslope, the danger is precisely the opposite in that, if the player does not align himself correctly to the slope and play

Downhill lie

the shot with it, he can all too easily dig in and kill the shot by taking far too much sand. Have the weight favouring the back foot and eschew the usual emphasis on keeping the club-face open through impact. In passing, it should be noted that there are golfers who pop the ball out off a steep upslope with a kind of perfunctory, sharp dunt into the sand.

When the feet are above the ball, whether the player is having to stand outside the bunker or not, bend from the waist, concentrate on balance and stay down on the shot. Remember to aim left because the shot will come out right. When the ball is above the feet, go down the grip, place even more stress than usual on making it more of a hands-and-arms shot, and aim right because the ball is going to emerge to the left.

There are all kinds of permutations of lie and stance, not least in respect of sheer faces and awkward lips, but mostly the normal golfing tenets allied to common sense will point to the percentage escape route. When you are practising, work on the

Uphill Lie

unusual bunker shots as well as the standard and find out, by trial and error, just what happens when you lay the face still more open and come into the shot at different angles.

As the distance increases – and the 30- or 40-yard bunker shot can be the most difficult to judge of all – the ball can be played farther back in the stance with the blade square. Again, do not forget that there is nothing in the rules to say that you have to use a sand-wedge.

As for the shot from a fairway bunker, the proximity and height of the lip or bunker face will mainly dictate what club you can sensibly use, always assuming that you have room for a full swing. Focus in addressing the ball on the need to take the ball before the sand and, above all, stay in balance.

Australia's Peter Thomson, after a memorable exhibition of sand play in winning the 1958 Open at the liberally bunkered Lytham, counselled golfers to swing almost more slowly through their bunker shots than they could believe. Gary

Uphill lie

Player, with the licence of a sand genius, attacks his bunker shots quite fiercely. All of which is just my way of suggesting that you find your own rhythm and tempo, the one stricture being that you go through the shot without that fatal deceleration.

It is part of the lore of golf how my distinguished compatriot, Tommy Armour, suggested to Julius Boros that he was such a good bunker player that he could afford to fire for the flag. There is a moral there.

Bernhard Langer has intermittently been troubled by the "yips" but for long periods has found salvation in the cack-handed grip, left hand below right.

SIXTEEN

PUTTING

There may be golfers who have successfully grooved putting strokes which at first felt awkward but I am definitely of the Bobby Jones school in that I think you have to feel comfortable at the address to putt well.

I always thought, too, that he was right in suggesting that attempting to copy slavishly the style of another, no matter how great a putter that model may be, merely induces an unnecessary and artificial tension. That is not to say that you cannot absorb into your own stroke little pointers you have picked up from the styles of other players, a classic instance of which occurred this year when Sandy Lyle found himself paired with Jack Nicklaus. Sandy noticed how Nicklaus really got down to the putt and, more specifically, how he set his right elbow at address so that it could act like a piston in the stroke. It is history how Lyle promptly went on to win the Greater Greensboro and the US Masters in successive weeks.

There are mechanical putters and those who rely to a greater extent on touch and feel but, of course, there is a bit of both about most of those who have been the greatest on the green. I should say myself that putters like Bob Charles and Ben Crenshaw were mechanical putters whereas, for all the repetitive soundness of his stroke, I always have the impression that Seve Ballesteros, as in all the other shots right through the bag, relies rather more on eye, touch and feel.

Interestingly, Bobby Locke was always held up by many as a

role model in respect of the unvarying ritual with which he set about a putt, with always the same two preliminary practice swings, no matter whether it was a three-footer in a bounce match or the last putt in an Open. Yet, interestingly, Locke, who flew in the last war, once told Cary Middlecoff that much though he would like to be able to switch to automatic pilot in the crunch moments of tournament golf, at such times, no matter the outward appearance, he was very much a touch and feel putter.

Anything that works on the greens is all right with me but, obviously, the more soundly based the method, the more chance it has of repeating and standing up to pressure. Today – partly, perhaps, through the influence of college golf in America in the not-too-distant past – putting techniques have tended to become more standardised.

In respect of the grip, the reverse overlap remains the most popular. Yet it is worth remembering that Bobby Locke, still held by many to be the most lethal of all time, stayed with his normal overlapping grip, save that he turned the hands so that both thumbs were pointing down the shaft and therefore the back of the left hand and the palm of the right square to the line of the putt at impact. There have, of course, been other much more extreme variations with England's David Snell winning the 1959 PGA Match-Play putting with his hands well apart, something which worked magically that week but almost immediately afterwards proved a recipe for disaster.

More and more players attempt to set up to the putt with everything square. It does have the advantage that that is an easy position to find and check. If you stand closed or open, there is always the question of just how closed or just how open you stood when you were last putting at your best.

Nevertheless, from time immemorial, many of the legendary demons of the green have stood either shut or open. One need only cite Bobby Locke whose closed stance was copied by his compatriot, Gary Player, and Jack Nicklaus, who stands open and who has possibly holed more putts which really mattered than any other golfer in history.

PUTTING

Head still has been seen by many as almost the basic tenet of good putting, and yet the freedom of movement which both Bobby Jones and Bobby Locke allowed themselves, with nothing held stationary, so struck Sam Snead that he hazarded that maybe we had all been on the wrong lines and would have done better to have been following suit. Perhaps that thought of Snead's would free some putters to sink a lot more putts than they have been doing but, to my mind, the reasoning behind keeping the head still in the putting stroke remains entirely valid for the great majority.

I am assuredly of the school who believe that there must be a hit in the stroke even if the style adopted is far removed from the rap putting of such as Bob Rosburg, Doug Ford and Billy Casper. That, in turn, implies a certain acceleration, the corollary of which is that deceleration into impact is liable to be fatal.

Innumerable authorities of impeccable credentials have argued for a shortening of the backswing to promote that acceleration, almost to force it, but, controversially or not, I see it as a dangerous notion. I am a great advocate of an ample backswing and would merely note, in passing, that almost the surest indication of the man who has "gone" on the greens is that he can hardly get the putter back before he has yipped the ball on its way.

There have been those who putted for the back of the hole: notably such men as Arnold Palmer and Tom Watson in their youth, when the prospect of holing the one back bothered them not a whit. But Locke, who declared that he had learned the art of applying topspin to a putt from Walter Hagen, always putted to allow the ball to die in the hole, thereby increasing the number of entrances. You could have called him a lag putter and not been too far wrong.

Many of the old-timers reckoned to take the club back with the left hand and hit with the right, but I have always suspected that that was less a matter of conscious application than of retrospective analysis.

Tommy Armour, a noted philosopher on the subject of putting, mused that the best putters had mostly been left-handed putters in the sense that that hand was the master hand. Many have attempted to lock the left wrist either by a raised left elbow as employed by such as Jerry Barber, who would surely have been mystified if you had told him he was borrowing from the principles of the classic forward defensive stroke in cricket; or by simply thinking of the left hand and wrist as being in an imaginary plaster cast. Lee Trevino went so far as to have actual casts made as a practice device to imbue the feeling he felt he should have.

I would endorse the thinking behind both and also, since they have the same end in mind, Bobby Jones's picture of the left hand going through towards the hole, Billy Casper's concentration on the back of the left hand holding square to the line of the putt and Bob Rosburg's determination never to allow the right hand to pass the left until after impact.

Yet, if there are few absolutes in the swing as a whole, there is scarcely one when it comes to putting and, in contrast, Bernhard Langer won the 1980 Dunlop Masters at St Pierre with a frugal expenditure of just 110 putts with his main putting peg to set the right hand at address and keep it locked in the same position through the stroke. Tony Lema, after advice from Horton Smith, became very much a right-hand dominant putter and was all the better for it.

There are celebrated tutors in America still teaching that the putter should go straight back and through as if within the confines of a miniature railway track, but I do not like it myself. Nick Faldo tried it at one time but eventually gave it away and now he visualises the putter "coming inside a hair on the way back and then straight through towards the hole on the line of the putt."

Much, of course, depends on the stroke: whether you see the putter face opening and closing as in the old image of a swinging gate, putt from shut to open à la Billy Casper, or perhaps simply see it as a modified version of the full golf swing. There have even been those such as Dave Douglas who holed out well with the sensation of cutting across every putt, but my own advice would definitely be to allow the putter to come inside at least on anything other than the very short putts.

As in the full swing, it has "already happened" before the follow-through, but that does not mean to say that there have not been plenty of golfers who hit the ball more squarely in their putting stroke by making sure that the putter-head went through towards the hole.

I preach that the putting stroke needs rhythm and flow no less than the golf swing itself, though how each man achieves that can be a very individual matter. For example, Bobby Locke, who always held his putter at the top of the grip even for the shortest putts, because he did not want to do anything that might alter the feel, was convinced that the putter should be held very loosely to promote a sensitive feel and looser still in a crisis. Yet as great a putter as Lloyd Mangrum, when he had a putt that really had to be holed, deliberately held the putter so tightly as to come within the white-knuckle grip so widely and mockingly condemned in respect of the so-called knee-knockers.

The choice of putter is a variation on the theme of one man's meat, but one thing I would say about my own preference for blade putters is that they make it easier, as it were, to cuddle a putt, though the very idea of doing so might be anathema to countless putting pundits.

Bobby Locke always maintained that you could tell a good putt by the sound it made, and perhaps within that conception lies just about the best tip of all – namely, to hit the ball solidly on the sweet-spot of the putter-face time after time.

At his peak, "the man who stooped to conquer", Michael Bonallack, used meticulously to marry at address the sweet-spot on his putter to the point on the ball he wanted to hit and, judging by the way he holed out, the only wonder is that that particular technique of his did not spread like the proverbial forest fire.

THE SHANK

The "professional" shank

Shanks can be caused by any one or more of a variety of swing flaws including both standing too near the ball and too far away – the latter the more common – and by swaying forward into the shot so that the hosel is pushed into the ball. What I call the "professional" shank is a high shank. It is usually caused by coming at the ball too much from the inside, frequently with the hands working independently of the feet, legs and body – and probably with the player having rolled the club flat on the backswing into the bargain. It can happen to all categories of golfer but, when it happens to the better player, it can frequently stem from a failure to release.

The "amateur" shank

The "amateur" shank, as I dub it, squirts away lower but equally embarrassingly with the ball trapped in the neck of the club. It can normally be traced back to coming over the top with the right shoulder coming excessively into the act. The soundest antidote to shanking is to concentrate on basics with a nice, rhythmic swing and natural cocking of the wrists, the head still but the lower body playing its role in terms of the movement into impact. Habitual shankers should repair to the practice ground and place a coin on the ground on the farther side of the ball. If they swing through without hitting the coin, they will not shank and it will teach them a lot about the swing path.

DRIVER SEQUENCE

Sam has almost always stood well to the ball, right foot virtually square to the line of play, left foot turned out but not exaggeratedly. The posture is technically very correct, yet relaxed to just the right degree.

The takeaway is orthodox with the clubhead a touch ahead of the hands. The left arm rotates but Sam is one of the players who, if he thinks too much about it, will overdo it and find himself more laid off at the top than suits his swing. I encourage him to be

Post-impact – the product of set-up and swing.

Address

Takeaway

Half-way back

Nearing the top

Above left, top of the swing.

Left, Sam Torrance showing a balanced, controlled finish.

Above right, starting down.

conscious of the left arm rotation in rehearsal, in his practice swing, but then to put it out of his mind for the shot itself. On the backswing, the left knee points in behind the ball but not to excess and the right hip clears. A flexed right knee provides the essential resistance to the body pivot in which the shoulder turn is a full 90 degrees and approximately twice that of the hip turn.

There are pupils who have to be encouraged to stress their shoulder turn but I have always been a devout advocate of a principle admirably expressed by the always articulate Tommy Armour – that you can turn the shoulders while keeping the hips fixed but that when you turn the hips, the shoulders almost have to go along.

All his career, Sam has tended to be a shade shut which is simply a characteristic integral to his swing and not a fault in itself, but it does mean that he has to hit a little "underneath himself".

He has great hands for golf, he has had since the day he first picked up a golf-club, but he makes almost no conscious use of them other than for special shots. The start down is very much in the hip and legs and, at his best, the behaviour of the right elbow on the downswing is a fine example for the club golfer. As previously noted, the image they should have is of compressing a giant sponge tucked in under their right armpit and Sam perfectly duplicates that action of the right elbow.

At impact, the right elbow is bent and so, too, is the right knee with the right foot adding its own push. The left side, the left arm and the left hand take the hit superbly and, of course, just as long as there is no breakdown there, it is impossible to hit too hard with the right hand. Sam has, too, the strength to use a certain supination of the left wrist for "type" shots.

His head is "quiet" rather than held rigidly still. It stays back as it should through impact and through Sam's copybook extension with both arms momentarily straight before the left arm begins to fold.

There is a lot of Ben Hogan's long right arm about Sam's swing as he moves on to a full and balanced finish in which the feet can be seen to have played their full part.

Overall, though, there is much more of Ben Hogan's legendary rival, Sam Snead, in my Sam's swing than there is of Hogan himself. But then, though I would reiterate that to me there has never been a better swing than Hogan's, nor one which gave birth to finer striking, I believe that Snead and even Jack Nicklaus are easier models for the great majority of golfers.

SEVENTEEN

THE YOUNG IDEA

Even in terms of when you take the game up, golf is the game of a lifetime but, for the record, players like my son, Sam, and Sandy Lyle were golfers, if not from the womb, then virtually from the cradle. Others, like Greg Norman and Nick Faldo, turned to golf in their mid-teens, while such as Larry Nelson, Calvin Peete and the great English lady amateur, Marley Spearman, were in their twenties before the game claimed them. Nevertheless, there are more advantages than otherwise to starting playing when very young, even apart from the fact that it is so great a game that the sooner you play, and the longer, the better.

Seve Ballesteros is a supreme case of a player who exhibits the natural feel for the game so often exuded by an inherently talented player who began very early. He is, too, living proof of how it pays, in terms of becoming a shotmaker, to have to improvise for the shot in hand rather than simply reach into the bag for the most appropriate club. Seve as a boy had just one club, a three-iron at that, with which to play every shot, including bunker recoveries and lofted pitches. The golfing imagination he shows to this day, and the sheer genius which goes into his manufacturing of unlikely shots, reflect the long hours of making that one-iron talk.

Even those parents or interested parties who deem restricting a youngster to just one club too extreme would still be wise to leave gaps in the set so that the boy or girl in question has to make up shots and learn to flight the ball and the dimension of bounce and roll.

Otherwise I contend that the most important thing is always to make sure, as I did with Sam, that the club the youngster is swinging has been cut down sufficiently and is not too long, or else he or she will be forced from the start into a swing which is much too flat, a fault which can be difficult to rectify later.

Because there have been some golfing legends from Arnold Palmer downwards who began with a grip which was much too "strong" but who subsequently succeeded in adjusting it, there is a school of thought that there is no need to be too fussy about a youngster's hold on the club in the early years. Better, surely, to keep it on the right lines from the first so that the hands come to settle on the club in the correct placement as if they had been born upon it.

Having dealt with the matter of the length of club and the youthful player's grip upon it, I personally reckon that the only other thing you have to do for them in those early years is exhort them to hit hard. Others see it the other way round, but no one will ever persuade me that it is not much easier to refine suitably a golfer who already hits the ball a long way than to add length to a golfer who has a good-looking swing but no hit.

Many a celebrated golfer owes most to the fact that he lived in his formative years hard by a golf course. As in other sports, ready access in the sense of somewhere to play is an invaluable ingredient in the evolution of a golfer.

Finally, I have always considered that formal instruction at an early age can all too easily be overdone, perhaps stifling flair or, worse, youthful enthusiasm. But never forget that small boys and girls are instinctively imitative and nothing will help more than playing much of their early golf in the company of those with good swings.

EIGHTEEN

SENIORS

Though he acknowledged that there were plenty of exceptions, the late Sir Henry Cotton subscribed to the view that on average a golfer lost a yard and a half in length for every year past his 40th birthday.

That, though, is a statistic which has been complicated by the fact that the ball now goes so much farther than once it did. Bob Charles declared at the Volvo Seniors' British Open at Turnberry that whereas, when he won the Open in 1963, a hole of 200 yards called for a two-iron or a three-iron from him, now at the age of 52 he would be reaching for merely a four or a five.

Nevertheless, even though the loss of length may now be for long enough only relative, the years do eventually eat tellingly into a golfer's yardage. In that respect, of course, those who play most have the best chance of holding the years at bay. Sam Snead, a marvel of golfing longevity, always said that the explanation with regard to how he kept his length as well as he did was that there was scarcely a day in his life when he did not play golf.

The phenomenal and remunerative growth of the American Seniors' tour has shown how much of the middle-aged decline in so many professional golfers of yesteryear was a matter of resignation stemming from a lack of incentive. Similarly, in amateur circles, even at club level, there are nowadays far more events for seniors.

The older player has now more reason to stay in shape and

Sam Snead, a marvel of golfing longevity.

Gene Sarazen, who was already a septuagenarian when he holed in one at Royal Troon's famous Postage Stamp in the 1973 Open Championship.

keep practising. Though it is probably true that for some veterans practising long hours can be counter-productive, the fact remains that Roberto de Vicenzo in his mid-sixties still often puts in over five hours' practice in the day and still hits the ball the healthiest of cracks.

Even in the more mature years, not every golfer is going to have the time for that kind of thing, even if he or she has the will and the desire. Yet they can do a great deal to keep their golfing muscles in trim and stop their swings from shortening expensively by swinging a weighted club as so fervently recommended by such legends of very different decades as Gene Sarazen and Gary Player.

As, sooner or later, the years inevitably begin to take their toll, the golfer can find the long irons more difficult to play and less rewarding than a five-wood or even a six-wood or seven-wood. Do not be too proud to make the change.

During the Seniors' championship at Turnberry, I found myself in agreement with Gary Player that the time-honoured advice to the senior golfer to switch to more flexible shafts can be taken too far, for it has to be borne in mind that, though they may restore a few yards, they are liable to lead to less control.

As the need to retain as much distance as possible becomes greater, even the better player has to give thought to switching to, say, the two-piece surlyn-covered ball, though it is not a switch to be made lightly. Bob Charles, for instance, is happy to give away some extra yards in order to benefit from the greater spin and feel inseparable from the softer-skinned balata cover. It all depends just how short you are and just how necessary to you those extra yards are.

On either side of the Atlantic, such leading luminaries of the senior scene as Neil Coles and Billy Casper have had to modify their actions as they found their bodies, and especially their legs and arms, moving less swiftly and willingly than in their youth. Yet, though it has long been said that it is the legs which go first, my own impression is that it is more often the eyes, and even Gary Player, who otherwise has withstood the years so well, now wears contact lenses.

SENIORS

One of the fascinations for the game's aficionados is that whereas there are countless elderly men and women who seem almost to putt better with the passing seasons, with the professional golfer nowhere is the mileage on the clock liable to show more damagingly than on the greens. I endorse the notion that the lively putters with a bit of rap in their stroke tend to last longest, but there is a lot in what Sir Henry Cotton used to say – namely, that the golfing mercenary has only so many three- and four-footers in him, and there comes a day when too many of them have been used up.

As the body begins to protest, good golf can still be played by making the clubhead do most of the work. Bing Crosby, with a dragging of the clubhead in the takeaway in a swing with a rhythm worthy of the Old Groaner, was still playing respectable golf till the day he died – fittingly after a round in Spain in which he had once more done his stuff.

The English professional, Laura Davies, who won the American Women's Open in 1987 and who drove 286 yards to the 292 yards of the former Amateur champion, Peter McEvoy, the first time they met in a long-driving competition.

NINETEEN

THE DISTAFF SIDE

It has become a golfing cliché that women, not having the strength of men, have to hit early, and that is why you so often see so many of them up on their toes at impact. Yet Bobby Jones, particularly when at full throttle off the tee, was also often caught up on his toes at impact.

No one ever doubted the muscle power of Bobby Jones for, from that leisurely swing of his, he generated great length. Pure timing, no matter how sweet, could never by itself account for the distance he obtained.

Jones, however, stood unusually close to the ball, and the explanation for his tendency to be up on his toes at impact, a tendency of which he himself disapproved, was reckoned by more than one knowledgeable pundit to originate in the need he felt instinctively to afford himself a little more room. Women, I have long argued, frequently have the same problem of getting out of their own way and making room for themselves, particularly those with bigger busts.

In that latter category, one would have to include the film star, Jane Russell, who still succeeded in becoming a useful golfer. But the Sabrinas and Barbara Windsors of this world are scarcely going to find it as simple as a flat-chested man to cultivate a free arm swing. They have, in my opinion, to become to a greater extent body players, with the downswing founded on a further dimension of the philosophy that if you can't beat 'em, join 'em.

Another familiar aspect of the teaching of women is that they should be given "strong" grips to facilitate the draw which will give them invaluable extra yardage. Once more, I do not much like it because, aside from the fact that if such a grip is overdone they will end up blocking out the prospective hook and hitting a fade, my own feeling is a good grip is a good grip. In other words, it is dangerous and possibly limiting to allow the grip a player takes to be dictated by gender.

Another popular fallacy is that women, being theoretically more delicate creatures than men, will have a better touch around the green and on it. In fact, weaker players tend to hang on for dear life to the exclusion of all feel, while some of the most powerful men in golfing history have demonstrated a pick-pocket's touch. It would seem that the easy hold born of great strength is an aid to delicacy. Indeed, I always find myself writhing in irritation when yet another television commentator marvels that some huge hitter does not display all the feel of a gorilla in boxing gloves.

As a sex in total, women are presumably never going to be as long and strong on a golf course as men but, especially since the growth of the women's professional tours in America and Europe, the scale of their golf would assuredly stand comparison with the male game of the rather more distant eras of the past.

There have always been, with regard to length, some formidable golfing Amazons, but even those who had known Babe Zaharias, Mickey Wright, JoAnne Carner and Nancy Lopez were more than a little startled to read that the former British Amateur champion, Peter McEvoy, had had to drive 292 yards to beat Laura Davies by a mere six yards at their first meeting in a long-driving contest.

As in other areas of life, knack and technique come into it as well as strength, and many of the golfing fraternity have heard of how, when the top of a jar has to be unscrewed in the household of Jack Nicklaus, he often has to hand it over to his wife, Barbara. By the same token, Tommy Armour used to love to tell how Lloyd Mangrum was always greatly puzzled by the strength his wife could generate in whipping a bowl of cream. Armour's notion was that the secret, as in long hitting in golf, lay in a certain lightness of grip.

The point is that innumerable women golfers are very far from helpless weaklings and, for my own part, I think that the distinction drawn between the teaching of the sexes is grossly exaggerated. Mostly, I teach them the same way and find that the seeds of good golf, the swing fundamentals, apply equally to men and women, boys and girls.

SLICE COMING UP

Having been the professional at a public course such as
Routenburn for a quarter of a century, I can vouch for the fact that
there is no more common malaise among longer handicap golfers
than an address position in which, probably because the ball is too
far forward, the shoulders are all wrong at the address with the
right shoulder already over and out. The set-up of the great
majority of chronic slicers.

Laid off   *Across the line*   *On line with target*

AT THE TOP

The aspiring golfer, who appreciates the advantages of a sound understanding of techniques in general and his own swing in particular, requires to understand what is meant by having the club laid off, across the line and to the target. None is wrong in itself while those who study still photographs should appreciate the pitfalls. The comparatively uninitiated looking at a picture of Bobby Locke half way up might think he was laid off whereas, by the time he had completed his backswing with a shoulder turn which Ken Bowden immortally likened to a wallowing whale, he is far across the line.

Those who are laid off require a pronounced lateral shift on the downswing to put the club on the correct inside plane coming back into impact. Though I always like to see the downswing starting downstairs, those who are across the line at the top can often get away with less activity below the waist than those who are laid off or even than those who are in what may fairly be deemed the optimum slot of straight to the target.

*The Ice-cold Kiwi. Bob Charles, the only left-hander to win the Open,
and a wonderful arm and shoulder putter over four decades.*

SUMMARY

Ben Hogan is regarded by the golfing fraternity at large as the finest striker the game has known: Jack Nicklaus, not least through the sheer weight of his record, as the greatest golfer overall. Yet to me they could hardly swing more differently. All of which is just to remind ourselves that there is no one way. Nevertheless, all else being equal, my role model:

Grip

Would grip with the club running diagonally across the palm of the left hand but with the hold of the right hand in the fingers; with the two hands married snugly in an overlapping grip; and with the Vs matching and pointing somewhere between the chin and the right shoulder.

Stance

Would have the right foot at 90 degrees to the line of play but the left foot turned out to between 30 and 40 degrees, the ball inside the left heel for all standard shots.

Posture

Would have the head up, the back straight but inclined forward from the waist, the posterior out and the knees flexed.

Takeaway

Would favour a one-piece takeaway or one with the clubhead just a little ahead of the hands.

Backswing

Would have the left knee pointing behind the ball; the right hip clearing; the right knee flexed and resisting; the shoulders turning till the left shoulder points at or behind the ball; and the left arm rotating to put the club "in the slot" at the top while encouraging a confidently wide backswing arc in which the right elbow could not fly.

Seve Ballesteros en route to winning the 1988 Open at Royal Lytham St Annes. The shot was from patchy rough, but what a gloriously free finish.

The Head

Would have a "quiet" head rather than one either held artificially stationary or allowed to rock, dip or rear.

Downswing

Would begin the downswing, however triggered, downstairs, in the feet, legs and hips, before the backswing has been completed, producing as the club changes into the downswing that invaluable touch of "cracking the whip".

Impact

Would have both the right knee and the right elbow bent rather than the former wrongly, and the latter prematurely, straightened.

Follow-Through

Would reflect in a balanced follow-through the free flow of a swing founded on correct and rhythmic footwork.

Like fingerprints, each player's swing is that little bit different. Nonetheless, if I am successful, the Bob Torrance signature on a pupil would always be the way he or she makes Room at the Top to time the downswing, the key to TEMPO.

Never Forget

FIRSTLY, that though there are many golfers playing very good golf with the sensation of coiling the upper half of the body against a resisting lower half, in the last analysis the top half can only do what the bottom half will allow

AND SECONDLY, that the more room you make at the top, the better you will time the downswing and the better you time the downswing, the better you will play.